EXTRA ORDINARY

CELEBRATING NEURO AND PHYSICAL DIVERSITY

THE ILLUSTRATOR

Violet Tobacco

Violet is an illustrator based in Atlanta, GA. Initially, Violet studied theater and performance studies. Over time, she grew to love the charm of storytelling above all else and jumped to illustration as a means to that end. In 2018, Violet became a full-time illustrator with representation from the Bright Agency. She has focused the last five years of her work on picture books, book covers, spot illustrations, and portraits. Still learning to navigate ADHD in her career, Violet has had the great fortune to work with other creative individuals that support and encourage her.

THE AUTHOR

Alicia Williamson

Alicia Williamson is an author and editor with a special interest in children's nonfiction. Since earning her PhD in English and Gender, Sexuality, and Women's Studies, she has worked as a university educator, community organizer, and chief editor at a feminist media startup. Whatever the context or medium, Alicia is dedicated to amplifying underrepresented stories and voices. Originally from the lake country of northern Minnesota, she now resides in the UK where she loves to decompress by foraging and fossil hunting with her border collie.

THE CONSULTANT

Josephine A. Lauren

Josephine A. Lauren (she/they) is a neurodivergent author and activist focused on mental health and social justice, specifically the safety and well-being of children. Her own story of recovery from childhood illness and trauma is published in over 30 magazines. Although Jo calls New York City home, she travels extensively, sharing her mental health journey along the way. You can review Jo's portfolio at www.josephineanne.com.

First published in 2024 by Welbeck Children's Limited
This edition published by Welbeck Children's Books
An imprint of Hachette Children's Group
Text and design © 2024 Welbeck Children's Limited

10 9 8 7 6 5 4 3 2 1
ISBN: 978 1 83935 297 3
Printed in Heshan, China

Welbeck Children's Books
An imprint of Hachette Children's Group
Part of Hodder & Stoughton Limited
Carmelite House, 50 Victoria Embankment
London EC4Y 0DZ
An Hachette UK Company
www.hachette.co.uk
www.hachettechildrens.co.uk

MIX
Paper | Supporting responsible forestry
FSC® C104740

EXTRA

ORDINARY

CELEBRATING NEURO AND PHYSICAL DIVERSITY

ALICIA WILLIAMSON

ILLUSTRATED BY VIOLET TOBACCO

WELBECK
CHILDREN'S BOOKS

CONTENTS

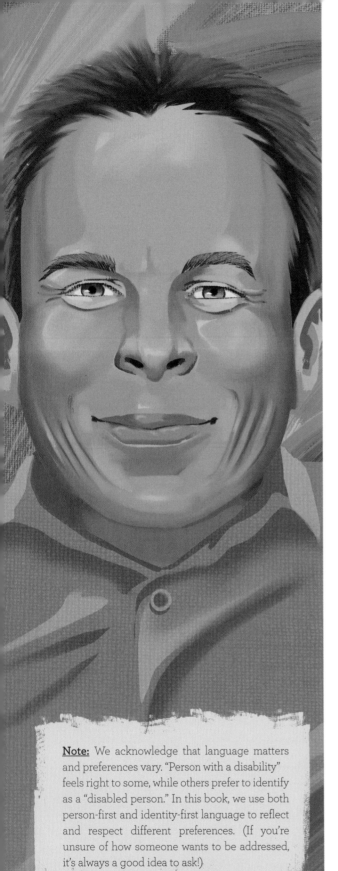

Introduction

Disabled and neurodiverse people have amazing, game-changing talents and abilities. You'll meet 25 of them in this book—ordinary, extraordinary people who have shared a range of experiences with disabilities and neurodivergence (or both!) with the world.

Disabilities and neurodivergence show that we all experience, think, learn, and interact with the world around us in different ways. Both are as diverse as we are. Some might be visible, while others not. In some cases, people are born with these unique attributes; while in others, they're the result of life-changing injuries and illnesses.

Either way, disabilities and neurodivergence are an ordinary part of life. Most of us will be impacted by one directly or indirectly. In fact, it's estimated that 15-20% of us have one or more mental or physical conditions that require additional sources of support to help us live healthy and happy lives.

If you're disabled or neurodiverse, parts of your body or brain might work differently than those of people without your condition/s. But, as the 25 people in these pages can attest, different doesn't mean less than. Inside this book you'll find stories of history-makers whose mental or physical conditions didn't stop them from building lasting legacies, like the trailblazing politician **Barbara Jordan** or the mighty theoretical physicist **Stephen Hawking**. And, you'll discover people—like animal scientist **Temple Grandin** or climate-change activist **Greta Thunberg**—who see their types of neurodivergence as not-so-secret "superpowers" that are helping them change the world.

We've also got athletes who've totally dominated their sports and accomplished unrivaled feats. Gymnast **Simone Biles** is arguably the greatest of all time, **Esther Vergeer** is a tennis hall-of-famer, and swimmer **Trischa Zorn** is the most decorated Paralympian in history. WCMX founder, **Aaron Fotheringham**, even invented a completely new sport: wheelchair motocross!

Many artists and entertainers have found that their disabilities or neurodivergence can spark creativity, like the famous abstract painter **Pablo Picasso** or musical theater star **Ali Stroker**—the first actor to use a wheelchair for mobility on Broadway. Movie-industry giant **Channing Tatum** found that a learning difference helped propel him toward the arts where he could excel by making the world his classroom. Meanwhile, actors like **Millicent Simmonds** and **RJ Mitte** are ensuring that disabled people can see themselves represented on screens—in all sorts of genres and storylines that don't necessarily revolve around disabilities.

Amy Purdy, a double amputee, and **Nick Vujicic**, who was born without limbs, have both tapped into their personal experiences of learning to thrive to coach and motivate others. **Michael J. Fox** and **Christopher Reeve** have used their Hollywood fame to advocate for those who share their conditions—and fast-track medical research—while A-list celebs like **Paris Hilton**, **Camila Cabello**, and **Billie Eilish** have destigmatized mental health conversations by speaking freely and positively about their own experiences to millions of fans. All of these stars have learned to rethink supposed limitations as opportunities in order to fulfill their dreams, then shared their outlooks outloud to support others.

In fact, many of these 25 people have used their successes to reshape societies where many continue to face barriers and discrimination, reinforcing that ALL people—especially those who are neurodivergent or have disabilities—are worthy of respect and inclusion. Together we can build a future that's better for everyone by treating each other well, standing up for one another, and celebrating—and accommodating—our differences.

Now turn the page, start reading . . .
and be EXTRAordinary!

Beyond incredible biographies, these pages also include short descriptions of the disabilities and types of neurodivergence mentioned. Look to these paragraphs to learn more about each condition.

PARIS HILTON

An entrepreneur, actor, model, reality
TV pioneer, and early social media wiz,
Paris Hilton has leveraged her privilege as
a weathly heiress to become a global celeb.
Known for her sensational style, Paris has
an influence that goes well beyond fashion.
Recently, she's used it to combat the stigma
surrounding ADHD by going public with
her own diagnosis. Far from seeing it as a
handicap, Paris credits the condition with
fostering the creative risk-taking that has
made her a huge success.

NAME: **Paris Whitney Hilton**

BORN: **February 17, 1981**

NATIONALITY: **American**

PROFESSION: **Entrepreneur and influencer**

An heiress to the ginormous Hilton hotel fortune, Paris Hilton has lived a supremely luxurious life. She spent her childhood being whisked between family mansions and A-list soirees. For her twenty-first birthday, she threw herself a party in five different cities around the globe. Her three-day wedding extravaganza featured seven couture gowns, including a see-through party dress made entirely of Swarovski crystal stars.

Her lavish lifestyle has led some people to dismiss Paris as an out-of-touch princess—and granted, tiaras are still one of her favorite accessories. Yet, being uncommonly privileged does not mean that her life has always been a fairy tale. Paris was diagnosed with ADHD as a kid and was put on medication for it at age 12. The mental health condition led to difficulties paying attention and impulsive behavior. In her teens, struggling under the glare of the spotlight, Paris acted out, skipped school, and partied so much that her parents sent her away to a boarding school that was part of what is now known as the "troubled teen industry." The four schools she attended were supposed to offer her specialized support that would help rehabilitate her. Instead, they traumatized her. She and the other students experienced daily physical and emotional abuse—including confinement, strip searches, and beatings—that continue to haunt Paris. (Today, she's an advocate for fellow survivors, ensuring these so-called "care" facilities have much-needed government oversight.)

Still, Paris battled back from the ordeal to become not only a major celebrity but a formidable mogul in her own right. She started by signing up with a reality TV show—one of the first of its kind. In 2003, she teamed up with her friend Nicole Richie for *The Simple Life*. The program, in which the socialites poked fun at their pampered lifestyles by attempting to do various kinds of manual labor, was so popular that it ran for five seasons. Paris emerged from it as a global influencer and early social media maven with her own trademarked tagline: "That's hot."

Since then, if there's something she's wanted to do, she's done it. She created her own production company to release her own self-titled pop album. She has modeled for top fashion houses and designed her own clothing collection. She has acted in several films and written best-selling books. She's even tried her hand at DJing. Paris's company includes 45 stores, 19 product lines, and 27 fragrances. And the multi-billion-dollar entrepreneur is also a big investor in up-and-coming brands.

In 2020, Paris revealed a new side of herself. A memoir and a YouTube documentary about her life (with 76 million views and counting) have exposed the complicated reality behind her lavish blonde party-girl persona. Cracking that shiny facade may just have made Paris a bigger influencer than ever—including when it comes to busting myths about ADHD. Yes, her ADHD means that her mind is always moving but not necessarily in a bad way. In fact, she believes that it keeps her dreaming up "new ways to do business," plus gives her the "drive and edge" to do so very many things so very well.

ATTENTION DEFICIT
HYPERACTIVITY DISORDER

Creativity, deep passion, and a focus on enjoyment are some of the many strengths of those with ADHD! Brains with ADHD attend to a number of things all at once, but may find it more challenging to focus on one thing. New and exciting experiences feel easy to engage in, while repetitive or uninteresting responsibilities prove more difficult. People with ADHD often enjoy moving around, talking, and daydreaming. So in spaces where they're expected to sit still, be quiet, and focus on something not of their choosing, it may be hard to follow the rules.

ADHD is common and often genetic, which means it is passed down by family. Those with ADHD can learn how to create a fulfilling lifestyle through the support, example, and advice of relatives and others who also share this condition. If you don't have ADHD, you can help those who do by encouraging and supporting them as they learn how to adjust to environments not designed to celebrate their strengths.

> " Life is too short to blend in. "
>
> PARIS HILTON

GRETA THUNBERG

CLIMATE CHANGE CRUSADER

Has something ever made you feel depressed—or kept you up at night? That's how Greta Thunberg felt about the climate crisis. Then, at 15, Greta decided enough was enough. She pitched a tent in front of Swedish parliament and began her first "school strike," demanding that the government take action to save her future. That personal protest set off a worldwide movement. The lesson? "No one is too small to make a difference."

NAME: *Greta Tintin Eleonora Ernman Thunberg*

BORN: January 3, 2003

NATIONALITY: Swedish

PROFESSION: Environmental activist

At one time, Greta Thunberg was an isolated kid with "no energy" and "no friends." But when she found meaning in fighting for a cause, she connected with millions. Now seen as the voice of her generation, the shy girl with braids has an influence so powerful it's called "The Greta Effect." Part of the reason she got there was learning how to work with her diagnosis of autism, turning what she initially experienced as a limiting condition into her not-so-secret superpower.

Greta was born into an artistic household in Stockholm, Sweden. Her father was an actor; her mother was an opera singer who once represented her country in the Eurovision Song Contest. Growing up with autism can make social interactions difficult, cause repetitive behaviors, and focus a person's interests. When Greta began learning about climate change around the age of eight, she soon became overwhelmed by it.

The loneliness and depression she felt began to lift when she made the decision to take action. Climate change became her special interest, and her autism kept her focused on achieving her goals! She started by lobbying her own family. They all turned vegan and stopped traveling by plane to cut down on their personal carbon footprints. Ready to make a bigger difference, she started camping out in front of the Swedish parliament three weeks before a big election in 2018. She wanted lawmakers to make good on their promises to lower emissions. At first, it was just her, holding a hand-painted sign that read "School Strike for Climate," but as more people joined in, it became an international news story. Many thousands of students around the world have joined in her Fridays for Future strikes since, and two multi-city protests have seen over one million kids take to the streets.

In fact, Greta led the largest climate protest in history following her famous speech at a 2019 UN climate event, where she condemned world leaders: "You have stolen my dreams and my childhood with your empty words. How dare you!" That same year, she was named *TIME* magazine's Person of the Year, the youngest ever individual to get this award. She also became an author who now has two books and a documentary, *I Am Greta*, to help spread her message.

Greta has credited her autism with empowering her to speak so directly and fearlessly about what she believes. She's called out decision-makers on their "blah blah blah" cheap talk everywhere, from the World Economic Forum to legislatures in the European Union, United States, United Kingdom, France, and Italy. Now, she's even suing her own government to uphold their climate pledges. She's also credited her autism with helping her deal with trolls—who've even included a few politicians. After all, she doesn't care about popularity, just justice. And take it from Greta: "When haters go after your looks and differences, it means they have nowhere left to go. And then you know you're winning!"

> ## " Being different is a superpower.
>
> GRETA THUNBERG

AUTISM

People with autism are on a spectrum, meaning that each individual has unique strengths and challenges. All autistic people show variations in how they communicate, relate to and understand others, learn and process information, move and feel their bodies, as well as experience and respond to what is happening around them.

Some focus deeply on specific interests, while others have excellent memories. One person may speak openly and honestly, while another will learn to communicate through body motions like sign language. Autistic people often prefer the same routine and have specific preferences for things like food and sensory experiences. They may practice stimming to express their emotions through movements like hand-flapping or making sounds such as humming.

While some autistic people can learn to live independently, others will need assistance from caregivers to manage their daily lives. Everyone is different and deserves to be loved and celebrated, so that they can live fully! If you have friends with autism, you can learn more about their preferences and the best way to support them by asking them or their loved ones.

CHRISTOPHER REEVE

SUPERMAN

Once upon a time, this high-flying actor was synonymous with DC's iconic red-caped superhero. Then, eight years after Christopher Reeve made his last of four *Superman* movies, his world came crashing down when an accident left him paralyzed below the neck. It took superhuman strength for Christopher to persevere, but he did—and became a true hero to those living with disabilities around the world.

NAME: *Christopher D'Olier Reeve*

BORN: **September 25, 1952**   DIED: **October 10, 2004** (age 52)

NATIONALITY: **American**

PROFESSION: **Actor**

Christopher Reeve was born into a well-to-do family in New York and raised in Princeton, New Jersey, by his mother after his parents got divorced. As a kid, he showed promise as an actor, joining local professional theater productions from the age of 15. After graduating from college, he trained at the prestigious Juilliard School where he was roomies with dear friend Robin Williams (who would later dedicate an Oscar to him).

Christopher's early career involved everything from appearing in a soap opera to touring with a Broadway show. Then, in 1978, he got his big break. Director Richard Donner took a chance on the relatively unknown Christopher to play the legendary title character in *Superman: The Movie*. He put on 30 pounds of brawn to join a cast that included Hollywood heavyweights like Marlon Brando and Gene Hackman. The film was the most expensive production in history at the time, but it grossed six times its budget at the box office, leading Christopher to don the form-fitting blue suit and red cape in three more movies, plus star in a host of other films.

With his silver-screen debut, Christopher became a legend and a pioneer of the hugely popular comic-book superhero genre. Off-screen, the actor's life was just as adventurous as his action-packed films. He was a licensed pilot and hang glider. He loved to sail, scuba dive, ski, and ride horses. Then, at a riding competition in 1995, Christopher was coming up to a triple-pole jump when his stallion Buck stopped, throwing him to the ground.

Christopher was so badly injured in the accident that he was paralyzed from the neck down. Confined to a wheelchair and forced to breathe with a respirator, he seriously considered allowing himself to die rather than living on life support. But his wife Dana helped him to see that, in spite of the traumatic changes to his body, he was still essentially himself. Together, they found a way for Christopher to continue his work in a way that created a much bigger impact than his time as Kal-El ever did.

In fact, for people with disabilities who saw Christopher striving valiantly to overcome his injury while fighting to improve the lives of others with similar challenges, he became a real-life Superman. Besides establishing a nonprofit that has raised millions for medical research on neurological conditions, Christopher lobbied on behalf of the disability community and created services that have helped more than 100,000 people and their families cope with life-changing injuries.

Christopher didn't give up on his film career, either. He acted in movies, got a two-minute standing ovation when he made a surprise appearance at the 1996 Oscars, and even took to the director's chair. Christopher died of heart failure at the age of 52, but his three children continue to lead the Dana & Christopher Reeve Foundation in honor of their heroic dad.

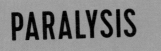

PARALYSIS

The spinal cord is the communication pathway between the brain and the nerves of the body, which allows people to feel and move. This pathway can be affected or disabled through physical injuries, strokes, or nerve conditions, causing paralysis—or the loss of the ability to move or feel in some or most parts of the body. Depending on the type of injury, some people will experience paralysis temporarily, then regain partial or full movement of their muscles over time, while others will live with paralysis for their entire lives.

Many people with paralysis utilize equipment and technologies to assist them in daily activities. Braces, wheelchairs, and driving devices allow for mobility, feeding appliances help with eating and drinking, voice-activated applications turn on lights, and communication devices promote speaking. If you have paralysis, you can connect with peers and families who can relate to your way of life. In order to help a friend with paralysis, just ask. Everyone can advocate for improved accessibility of public environments for people with paralysis, so we can all enjoy them together!

"

A hero is an ordinary individual who finds the strength to persevere and endure in spite of overwhelming obstacles.

"

CHRISTOPHER REEVE

19

SIMONE BILES

GYMNASTICS G.O.A.T.

Simone Biles is an absolute legend. She is a 4-foot-8 powerhouse who vaulted to fame by winning her first World Championship at 16, then won four more, a seven-times Olympic medalist, and the most decorated gymnast of all time. Her daring to push the limits of her sport is matched only by the personal courage she's shown beyond it—by candidly speaking out about ADHD, mental health, and surviving abuse.

NAME: *Simone Arianne Biles*
BORN: March 14, 1997
NATIONALITY: American
PROFESSION: Gymnast

According to the Gymnastics Code, if you're the first person to successfully perform a move in competition, it'll be named after you. There are FOUR named "Biles." They include skills like a triple-twisting double somersault—moves so gravity-defying, it's uncertain if anyone else will be able to pull them off again. Still, it has to be said that some of Simone Biles' most inspiring moves have taken place off the mats. Time and time again, this gymnast has faced up to challenges to become not only a champion in her sport but a champion for kids everywhere who face adversity on the way to achieving their big dreams.

Simone was born in Ohio but brought up by her grandparents in Texas. Her biological parents weren't equipped to raise children, so Simone and her siblings were put into foster care before being adopted by family members. As a child, Simone was diagnosed with Attention Deficit Hyperactivity Disorder (ADHD), a condition that can make it difficult to concentrate without the help of medication. However, when you have a serious passion for something, ADHD can actually lead to super focus and determination. And Simone did have a passion.

On a daycare field trip to a local gymnastics studio at the age of six, Simone tumbled upon the sport that would give her a purpose. It was the perfect way to channel her energy, and soon she was training 30+ hours a week to become an elite competitor. She made her debut on the senior circuit in 2013, taking home the national and world titles while becoming a crowd favorite for the sheer exuberance she brought to performing her routines and cheering on teammates.

With 14 world medals already under her belt, expectations were high for the 2016 Summer Olympics in Rio. As the pressure mounted, Simone wanted to be clear: "I'm not the next Usain Bolt or Michael Phelps—I'm the first Simone Biles." And make a name for herself she did, tying the record for the most gymnastics medals won in a single Games. Plus, four of the five were gold!

In the wake of her historic win, hackers leaked Simone's private medical records. They questioned her use of the ADHD treatment Ritalin as a potentially performance-enhancing drug. The superstar flipped the script on her critics, tweeting: "Having ADHD and taking medication for it is nothing to be ashamed of, nothing that I'm afraid to let people know." When the story broke that a team doctor for USA Gymnastics had been abusing gymnasts, Simone came forward as one of 300 survivors. She acknowledged the pain she was working through and vowed not to let one man "steal her love and joy." Her powerful public statement prompted the team to cut ties with the training facility where the abuse took place.

When the 2020 Olympics finally arrived, the world was waiting for the 24-year-old Simone to top the podium again. But this time, there was a twist. A mental block called "the twisties" was making aerial moves difficult. In spite of the pressure to secure her legacy and help her team to gold, Simone bravely prioritized her mental health and personal safety. She withdrew from the team competition and four event finals but battled back to win an individual bronze on the beam—perhaps the medal she's most proud of.

"I'D RATHER REGRET THE RISKS THAT DIDN'T WORK OUT THAN THE CHANCES I DIDN'T TAKE."

SIMONE BILES

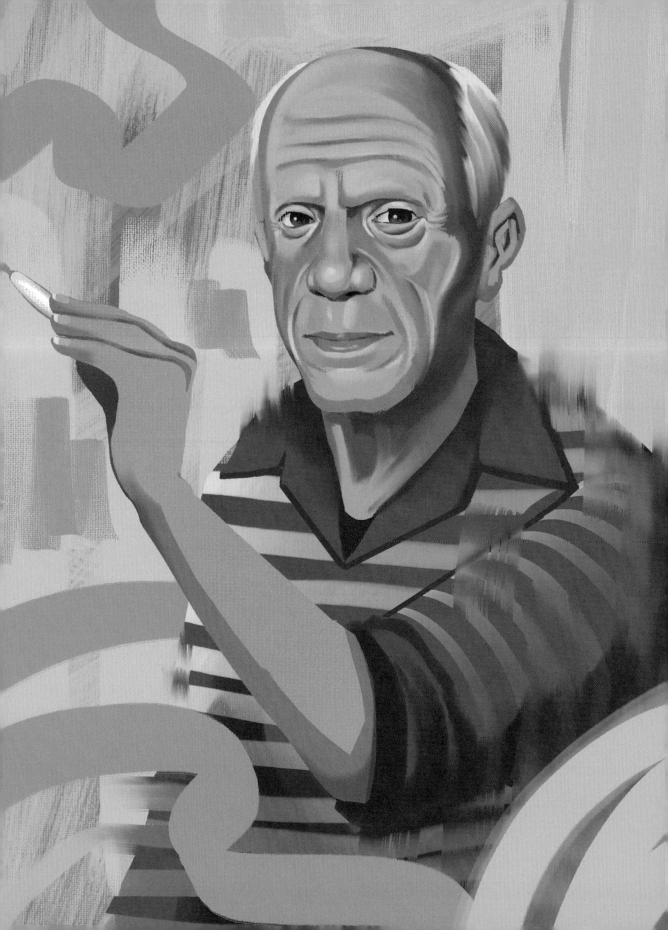

PABLO PICASSO

ARTIST EXTRAORDINAIRE

Pablo Picasso is famous for his inventive,
unconventional, eye-boggling art.
Yet, part of his genius was showing the
world as he often saw it—backward,
rearranged, from multiple angles at once.
You see, Picasso had dyslexia.
This learning difficulty made school
a real challenge, but it also helped spark
the visionary creativity that has made
Picasso one of the world's
best-known painters.

NAME: *Pablo Ruiz Picasso*

BORN: October 25, 1881   DIED: April 8, 1973 (age 91)

NATIONALITY: French

PROFESSION: Artist

Born in Malaga, Spain, Pablo Picasso was a terrible student growing up. Teachers concluded he had "reading blindness." Letters would move around on the page as he tried to read and write, a symptom of a condition that we now recognize as dyslexia. Frequently sent out of the classroom as punishment for his poor work, Picasso would spend the downtime doodling. As it turned out, he had a real knack for it.

Eventually, his father, who was a professor of drawing, took a job at Barcelona's School of Fine Arts, so that his son could enroll. Picasso started there at age 14. The following year, one of his academic paintings got an honorable mention in Madrid's Fine Arts Exhibition. While Picasso moved to a more prestigious academy to please his father, he soon decided he was done with formal training. He didn't want to master old techniques; he wanted to revolutionize them according to his unique perspective.

He dropped out of The Royal Academy of San Fernando and headed for Paris with a friend. The City of Light was a hub for modern artists who were pushing the boundaries of their fields. Picasso became a major player among them. A painter, sculptor, printmaker, and potter, he experimented with multiple styles. Along the way, he helped found an artistic movement—Cubism. Starting in 1907, he and a French artist, Georges Braque, began bringing together multiple views of the same subject within a single painting. The result was the disorienting and fascinatingly abstract pictures we've come to associate with Picasso, pictures that don't follow the "normal" rules of realistic representation. Picasso already knew from his schooldays that his experience wasn't the same as others. Now, he was picturing a "new reality" for the world to experience his vision of modern life.

During World War I, Picasso added set designer to his resume. He created a realistic backdrop to contrast wildly abstract Cubist costumes for Jean Cocteau's modern ballet *Parade*. Picasso met his first wife among the production's dancers and continued to collaborate with the show's dance company, the Ballet Russes, into the 1920s.

In the lead-up to World War II, Picasso created one of his most iconic works, the mural *Guernica*. Named for a Spanish town bombed in 1937 by Fascists (authoritarian forces), the painting was displayed at the Paris World's Fair on behalf of the democratic forces who were fighting against Fascism in his native country. Its dark imagery denounced dictators and the violence of war.

Unlike many artists, Picasso's works already fetched big money during his lifetime. In fact he bought a castle where he could store the 50,000 works he kept for his personal collection. He was so prolific, estimates put his total output at 147,800 pieces, including 13,500 paintings. In spite of the thousands available, Picasso masterpieces continue to sell for tens of millions—a mark of just how influential he's been on modern art.

"

The world today doesn't make sense,
so why should I paint pictures that do?

"

PABLO PICASSO

DYSLEXIA

Do you or one of your loved ones have dyslexia? If so, activities like problem solving, puzzles, and building things may feel fun and natural, while other tasks like reading, writing, and doing math may be more challenging.

Those with dyslexia use different areas of their brains to process letters and numbers. They need extra tools to help connect the sounds of the letters and numbers that they hear with the shapes of the letters and numbers that they see on the page. With time, practice, patience, and support, this process can become easier, making reading, writing, and math more enjoyable.

Learning with dyslexia can be fun! Listening to audiobooks, playing educational games, and writing with computers will all support reading, writing, and math goals. Dyslexia is common, so connecting with other kids who have it can also be helpful. Remember to be patient with yourself and others, since everyone excels at new skills at a unique time and pace. Always focus on what you enjoy, and celebrate your strengths!

BILLIE EILISH

SENSATIONAL SINGER-SONGWRITER

Billie Eilish burst onto the music scene at age 15 when her haunting vocals went viral. By 18, she was a record-breaking Grammy winner. But her undeniable talent isn't the only reason for her meteoric rise. She's earned millions of fans with her unique style, authentic personality, and open-book attitude— even when it comes to discussing dark or challenging topics.

NAME: *Billie Eilish Pirate Baird O'Connell*

BORN: December 18, 2001

NATIONALITY: American

PROFESSION: Singer-songwriter

When Billie Eilish was growing up in Los Angeles, she and her older brother Finneas were homeschooled. Her actor parents wanted to give their kids the space to focus on creative expression. Turns out that was a very smart decision, because they ended up raising a pair of creative geniuses who had already left their mark on the music industry by the time they were teenagers.

The young Billie used her freedom to ride horses, dance, and take gymnastics. She played ukulele, sang with a children's chorus, and performed Lana Del Rey songs at talent shows. Billie began songwriting at age 11—the same year she was diagnosed with Tourette's syndrome, a neurological disorder that caused her to have physical tics, or sudden, repeated movements such as raising an eyebrow and clicking her jaw. Having constant tics was exhausting, but she found that focusing on an activity like singing helped control them.

When Finneas—who's also responsible for his sister's awesome middle name "Pirate"—asked a 13-year-old Billie to sing on a track he'd written for his own band, the song, "Ocean Eyes" went viral. A record label raced to sign her. Then Billie hit it out of the park with her debut album, the 2019 *When We All Fall Asleep, Where Do We Go?* With the help of her dance-pop megahit "Bad Guy," Billie proceeded to become the youngest artist ever to top one billion streams on Spotify and to sweep all the music industry's top honors at the Grammys—including song, record, and album of the year.

Since then, she's notched up seven Grammys, played the biggest festivals from Glastonbury to Coachella, and even taken home an Oscar and Golden Globe for her brilliant James Bond theme song "No Time to Die" (another collab with her brother!).

Billie has won countless fans with standout performances but also because she's always stood out as being brave enough to be herself. Known for her oversize clothes, memorable style (including her once slime-green roots), and edgy-yet-relatable lyrics, Billie broke the mold of your typical pop songstress. Yet with the adoration has come unwanted attention. When video compilations of her tics began to surface on social media, she was forced into revealing her diagnosis. She set the record straight with grace, humor, and honesty about her struggles. Her willingness to speak publicly about her Tourette's and other challenges she's faced, like depression and self-harm, have inspired others to break their silence on taboo subjects.

While she initially didn't want to speak about her Tourette's because she didn't want it to define her, today she's come to embrace it as a key part of who she is. According to Billie: "I have made friends with it. And so now, I'm pretty confident in it."

TOURETTE'S SYNDROME

Tourette syndrome (TS) causes repetitive, uncontrollable movements and sounds called tics. Tics can include blinking, head jerking, and jumping, as well as vocal noises like whistling, clicking, and shouting. Certain emotions can cause tics to increase such as feeling nervous, upset, excited, sleepy, or hungry. Many people with TS report that being focused on an activity can help to reduce tics. Tics often change over time and can subside for certain periods of time.

If you have TS, you can practice taking ownership of your tics and surrounding yourself with those who accept them, too! Teaching your peers about your tics may empower you, while inviting others to be understanding and supportive. Those who don't have TS can assist loved ones by being patient with how they express themselves, ignoring tics if they interrupt conversations, and defending your friend or family member if they are being questioned or mistreated. Together, we can all learn to love and accept each other better!

"

I'm not going to say I'm cool, because I don't really feel that. I just don't care at all, and I guess that's what people think is cool.

"

BILLIE EILISH

ANDREA BOCELLI

STANDOUT SINGER

What do you get when you mix classical opera with pop music? Popera! And this renowned tenor is one of the all-time masters of the genre. The golden-voiced Andrea Bocelli has turned arias into hitmakers, dueting with everyone from Celine Dion to Jennifer Lopez. Visually impaired since childhood, he credits his blindness with giving him the supersensitive ear that has helped make him a music legend.

NAME: *Andrea Bocelli*

BORN: **September 22, 1958**

NATIONALITY: **Italian**

PROFESSION: **Opera singer**

Today, singer Andrea Bocelli does not see his blindness as a disability. It has given him a sense of hearing so sharp that he can click his fingers and know how far away a wall is. It has helped him excel as a musician and given him the wherewithal to overcome obstacles. Still, learning to cope with visual impairment was often tough when he was growing up on his family's farm in Italy. Andrea was born with congenital glaucoma (a condition resulting in limited vison caused by fluid buildup in the eye damaging the optic nerve.). He spent a lot of time in hospitals as a kid, with doctors trying to rescue what vision he had left.

When he was five, his mother noticed that turning classical music on gave her young son comfort when his illness or treatments were getting him down. Even though the rest of his family showed no great interest in music, Andrea soon developed a passion for it. He memorized all the arias from the Verdi opera *Il trovatore* by the time he was six. He had already learned to play multiple instruments—piano, flute, saxophone—when at age 12 an accident stole his remaining sight. A ball smashed into the one eye he could still see with during a soccer game. The impact was so fierce, it caused a brain hemorrhage. Doctors tried operation after operation, but nothing helped. Andrea was now completely blind.

Music helped Andrea adjust to his new reality with courage. He learned how to read notes through braille and began entering local talent contests. He worked his way through a law degree by singing at nightclubs and piano bars. But a year into his legal career, he changed his tune to chase his musical passion full time.

Andrea signed up for every audition and contest he could find, struggling to get noticed. Then, in 1994, he won Italy's most famous televized song competition, the Sanremo Music Festival. His record score led to a major record deal. National recognition quickly blossomed into international fame with his multiplatinum single "Time to Say Goodbye," and his 1997 album *Romanza* became one of the best-selling of all time.

Since then, Andrea has become a true pop maestro. His 17 studio albums and multiple hit records have sold more than 80 million copies worldwide. He has won a Golden Globe for best original song and earned a star on the Hollywood Walk of Fame. He has performed for royalty, popes, and heads of state and shared the stage with pop divas such as Christina Aguilera and classical giants like Luciano Pavarotti. He has even starred in traditional operas, from *La Bohème* to *Madame Butterfly*. His nontraditional style has led to criticism from the classical music world, but that hasn't kept Andrea from nabbing the world record for the best-selling classical album by a solo artist with *Sacred Arias*.

In 1999, Andrea published an autobiographical novel called *The Music of Silence*, which in 2017, was made into a film about the blind singer's thorny path to stardom. Even people who aren't moved by Andrea's blow-you-over emotional vocal performances have been touched by his inspiring story.

> Music touches the soul, it stirs passion, it moves us and can make us better people.

ANDREA BOCELLI

GLAUCOMA

The optic nerve carries messages from the eye to the brain, allowing people to see. Glaucoma occurs when fluid buildup in the eye damages the optic nerve and limits a person's vision or causes complete blindness.

People with low vision or blindness learn specific skills through other senses and tools. Some use sighted guides, white canes, or trained dogs to understand the orientation of things, detect obstacles, and safely navigate their environments. Reading occurs through braille—a system of characters represented by raised dots—and screen readers that transmit computer text into tactile or auditory messages.

Blind or low vision people organize their environments and routines into memorized sequences, advancing their memory skills. Many are excellent listeners and communicators since they rely on sounds and language to interact with others instead of visual cues. If you are a sighted person, you can support people who are blind or with low vision by asking what they need and communicating clearly before approaching or touching them.

MILLICENT SIMMONDS

BREAKOUT KID STAR

Have you ever just gone for something, even if it was a long shot? That's what Millicent Simmonds did when, with zero professional acting experience, she answered an open call for a deaf actor about her age. Her daring paid off. She scored a part in a Hollywood film, opening the door to a glittering career while paving the way for other disabled actors in the industry.

NAME: *Millicent "Millie" Simmonds*

BORN: March 6, 2003

NATIONALITY: American

PROFESSION: Actor

Millicent Simmonds was born in Bountiful, a small city in Utah. Just before she turned one, she received an overdose of medication that left her deaf. Millie eventually got a cochlear implant that restored some of her hearing, but she didn't really mind being deaf. Her mother was very supportive, she learned American Sign Language (ASL) and taught the whole family to keep Millie from feeling isolated.

Communicating with ASL is about more than just words. It also involves body language and facial expressions—perfect preparation for acting. Millie loved connecting with others by telling stories with her hands. She enthusiastically joined the drama club at her school for deaf children. Her first big role was playing the rascally fairy Puck in Shakespeare's *A Midsummer Night's Dream*.

Millie adored acting, but it never occurred to her that she could do it professionally. She'd never seen a deaf actor on the big screen before. As it turned out, she would go on to become that actor.

When her drama teacher saw an audition notice, she encouraged Millie to try out. The casting agents were looking for a deaf actor around her age to star in an adaptation of the novel *Wonderstruck*. Millie's tape—filmed on her mom's smartphone—was one of 200 sent in. It brought director Todd Haynes to tears. Needless to say, the 12-year-old got the part and soon found herself on set with the likes of Julianne Moore and Michelle Williams (both Oscar-nominated actors!). Before she knew it, Millie was walking her first red carpet for the movie's premiere at the Cannes Film Festival—and absolutely loving it. She knew she wanted to stay in this industry. The industry felt the same way about her.

Millie went from period mystery to sci-fi horror flick with her casting in the 2018 *A Quiet Place*. The plot follows a family who must live in silence to avoid being hunted down by monsters with supersensitive hearing. When director and star John Krasinski asked Millie to be in the film, he got not only an actor but also a trusted consultant. She taught her costars ASL, weighed in on the story, and helped solve the problem of how to make a mostly silent movie so compelling. The film ended up being both a critical and box office success, racking up rave reviews and grossing $340 million globally. She also helped ensure that the 2020 sequel was just as good as the original.

Lauded as one of the most gifted child actors of her generation, Millie continues to bring inspired representations of deaf experience to screen and stage. She even began producing her own projects—like the adaption of *True Biz*, the Sara Nović novel set in a deaf school—while she was still in her teens. She has become a visible advocate for her community and for on-screen diversity. What she'd really like to see is more representations of disabled people that don't focus on them struggling to cope with their disability. "Send them up to space, have them in a love story," she says, "Doing things that other people are doing."

DEAF, DEAFENED, HARD OF HEARING

People who are deaf or hard of hearing often use their senses of sight and touch to interact with others because they have limited or no ability to hear sounds. Some people are born deaf or hard of hearing, while others become so due to illness or physical trauma. There are a number of tools that deaf and hard of hearing people utilize to manage and enjoy their lives.

Many people practice sign language—a communication style that uses hand shapes, as well as hand and body positioning and movements, to convey words and tell stories. If wanted, hearing aids or cochlear implants can be attached to their ears to amplify sounds and transmit messages to their brains that may be understood over time through practice and therapy. Assistive listening tools within phones or on screens can make voices louder or transform speech into written words.

If you are deaf or hard of hearing, you can share your communication preferences with your loved ones. Hearing people can make listening easier for those who are deaf or hard of hearing by speaking one at a time, facing forward, using visual cues, and clearly articulating words. Also consider learning sign language so that you can communicate in a number of ways!

"

There will always be people who won't accept you, but there are others you can find who will. You're never alone.

MILLICENT SIMMONDS

GARY PAYTON II

LATE-BREAKING BASKETBALL STAR

If you had a big dream, how long and how hard would you work to make it happen? After being dropped from five pro teams before he even got a chance, Gary Payton II was about to move to Plan B when he suddenly scored a spot on the roster—of a title-winning NBA team! Gary's early experiences with dyslexia helped him persevere to dribble, press, and steal his way to hoops greatness.

NAME: *Gary Dwayne Payton II*
BORN: December 1, 1992
NATIONALITY: American
PROFESSION: Pro basketball player

"I realized young I was a late bloomer," says Gary Payton II. But in case anyone doubts it: "Gains *are* going to come."

Gary was the first son of two basketball players. His dad, Gary "The Glove" Payton, was one of the legends of the game. Gary II grew up under the shadow of the Seattle SuperSonics superstar, avoiding basketball altogether so he could avoid the expectations heaped on him.

Throughout his childhood, Gary struggled with self-confidence. While his siblings did well in school and sports, he appeared uninterested in both. Then in second grade, Gary was diagnosed with dyslexia, a learning difference that can hinder reading, spelling, and understanding language. At first, the diagnosis pushed Gary further into his shell. He didn't want anyone in his class to think he was different. He dreaded reading aloud. He avoided asking or answering questions and fell behind because it was difficult for him to follow ideas when teachers explained them verbally.

Slowly, Gary learned to adapt. He began speaking up and asking for the help he needed. If he didn't catch something in class, he would approach the teacher after to make sure he got it. At the same time, Gary unlocked his hidden passion for basketball.

Already in junior high, he was starting late, for sure. Gary made up for the years he'd missed by working three times as hard. When high school graduation rolled around, three colleges offered him a basketball scholarship—but he didn't have the grades necessary to enroll. So, Gary adapted again, going to a preparatory school and putting in time at a community college till he qualified to become a starter at Oregon State.

Gary came away from his college career as a two-time Pac-12 Defensive Player of the Year. Still, no pro teams opted to draft him. Some might have let self-doubt put an end to their dream of playing in the NBA there. Not Gary. He agreed to sign with the Rio Grande Valley Vipers in 2016 and bounced around the NBA's Development League the next several years.

The 6-foot-2 guard had already been temporarily signed and cut from five NBA teams. Then in 2021, at the age of 29, Gary finally got the break he deserved. It happened because he kept on showing up.

Players at the Golden State Warriors had convinced the management to grant Gary three short-term contracts. But it looked like he was going to be waived again before the season opener, so Gary met with the assistant coach to see if he could stay on by taking a job in the team's video department. Instead, he locked down the fifteenth and last spot on the team roster. How'd his first season as a legit pro go? It was a slam dunk. Gary helped the Warriors cruise to an NBA Championship title.

Today, Gary is widely acknowledged to be one of the top defensive guards in basketball. As a visual learner, he's especially good at absorbing lessons from video. It's helped him neutralize some of the games' biggest threats and stuff players that are way taller than him. (He's even learned some cool moves by watching videos of his dad from 20 years ago!) The story of "Young Glove" is reason to believe: Gains will come when you adapt to setbacks but stay the course.

STAY THE COURSE IS THE MOTTO, FOR SURE. IT'S GOING TO BE BUMPY. IT'S GOING TO HAVE POTHOLES AND DIRT ROADS OR WHATEVER IT MIGHT BE, BUT STAY THE COURSE.

GARY PAYTON II

CAMILA CABELLO

POP SUPERSTAR

Have you ever needed help but found it hard to ask? On the surface, singing sensation Camila Cabello seemed to be living a dream come true, which made it tough to admit even to herself how much she was suffering with anxiety. Being brave enough to audition for *The X Factor* had changed her life. Being brave enough to talk about the OCD symptoms she was experiencing saved her life—and gave others the courage to say those essential words: "I need help."

NAME: *Karla Camila Cabello Estrabao*

BORN: March 3, 1997

NATIONALITY: **American**

PROFESSION: **Singer-songwriter**

At 15 years old, Camila Cabello—the shy girl who used to cry when her parents asked her to sing for them—faced down her fears and auditioned for the reality TV competition, *The X Factor*. She got the idea because she was a massive "Directioner"—aka, a big fan of the boy band One Direction who'd got their start on the show. Little did she know that she would soon become part of another of producer Simon Cowell's dream teams. Though Camila didn't make it through to the finals on her own, she was invited to join up with four other contestants. Their girl group Fifth Harmony took third in the 2012 competition and scored a record deal in the process. Like "1D," "5H" turned out to have a serious "X factor."

All of a sudden, Camila was out of high school and into the music industry. She took the lead on hit singles like "Worth It" and "Work from Home," put out three albums, sang twice at the White House, and toured nonstop. When she went solo as a singer-songwriter in 2016, her career soared higher still. Camila's breakout single "Havana"—inspired by the Cuban hometown her family left behind for Miami, Florida, when she was six years old—topped charts around the world. She collaborated with the likes of Ed Sheeran and Shawn Mendes; she opened for the likes of Bruno Mars and Taylor Swift. After her first two albums went platinum, she began headlining her own arena shows and became a streaming powerhouse with billions of listeners. She even made her film debut in a new musical version of *Cinderella*.

On stage and screen, Camila shone, but behind the scenes, she was suffering with mental health issues—and trying to keep them in the dark. As a teen, she had been diagnosed with obsessive-compulsive disorder (OCD). OCD is an anxiety condition that can cause repetitive thoughts and behaviors, which often seem uncontrollable. Camila frequently felt like her "mind was playing a cruel trick" on her, overwhelming her with negative thoughts, and it was affecting her body, too. Her heart raced all the time, and she had chronic headaches. Sometimes she would sleep all day, and sometimes she couldn't sleep at all. During one Fifth Harmony concert, she had to walk off mid-performance due to an anxiety attack.

Still, with so much success, Camila felt "embarrassed," "ashamed," and even "ungrateful" when OCD symptoms appeared. She didn't want to admit that her private experiences didn't always match her confident public persona. But in 2020, Camila tapped into the same bravery that first took her to the stage to put mental health awareness in the spotlight. "There was something hurting inside me," she wrote in an editorial about her OCD journey, "and I didn't have the skill to heal or handle it. In order to heal it, I had to talk about it."

Camila realized that she had to start showing up each day, not just for her fans but for herself. OCD is still with her, but she has learned how to use therapy, daily meditation, and breath work to manage the toughest symptoms. She's also learned to use her fabulous voice to back other issues that matter to her, like climate action, girls' education, and immigrant rights.

> " The only way to experience magic is to believe in it.

CAMILA CABELLO

OBSESSIVE COMPULSIVE DISORDER

People with obsessive compulsive disorder (OCD) have worry thoughts and actions. For example, they may feel anxious about a loved one getting sick, being hurt, or dying. For some, fear of germs can make them feel dirty, while others may need objects to be ordered in a specific way. Worry thoughts like these feel sticky to people with OCD because they remain in the brain and will not leave. Worry actions are things that people with OCD do to cope with fear. They may clean themselves repeatedly, redo something over and over again, or organize their things in a preferred way.

Therapy, encouragement, and reassurance can be helpful for those with OCD. They can learn to listen to their fears without believing that they are true, then practice coping activities that actually make them feel better such as positive self-talk. OCD might not go away, so people with this condition learn to be brave, as they practice doing things even though they are anxious and afraid. If you or a loved one have OCD, together you can celebrate courage constantly!

ESTHER VERGEER

TENNIS LEGEND

For more than a decade, Esther Vergeer held total domination over her sport. In fact, when she retired from wheelchair tennis in 2013, she hadn't lost in her last 470 matches. Esther the Invincible's astonishing winning streak raised the profile of Paralympic sports and inspired people around the world— including kids like her, learning to survive and thrive in the face of life-altering medical conditions.

Esther Vergeer

BORN: July 18, 1981

NATIONALITY: Dutch

PROFESSION: Tennis player

One day, when Esther Vergeer was just six years old, she began to feel dizzy and passed out. Doctors could see she had bleeding and a build-up of fluid around her brain, but they couldn't see the cause. After she experienced a stroke at age eight, they discovered there was a defect in the blood vessels around her spinal cord. An operation fixed the problem but left her paraplegic—paralyzed from the waist down.

At first, Esther was devastated. She looked out the windows from her family home in Woerden, Netherlands, and thought about all the things she couldn't do anymore—even simple things like running around outside. But her parents wouldn't let her give up. Instead, they encouraged her to rebuild her confidence and joy in life by trying things she'd never done before.

Esther wasn't especially sporty as a young kid, but athletics became an important part of her recovery. She learned how to play basketball and tennis in a wheelchair. With each shot swished and landed, her physical and mental strength grew. She worked so hard to improve, that she was competitive in both sports by the time she was a teenager.

In 1997, she helped the Dutch national team win the European championship for basketball. Soon after, she decided to dedicate her gold-medal mindset solely to tennis. Playing in a custom-built wheelchair nicknamed "Quickie," Esther was commanding the courts within a few short years. With her wicked backhand and 78-miles-per-hour service, she began to rack up trophies and medals.

She took home 44 Grand Slam titles and seven Paralympic golds. She held down the number-one ranking for 13 years in a row and twice won the hugely prestigious Laureus World Sports Award for players making a global impact.

Yet, the more Esther won, the greater the pressure became to never drop a game. At 32, she decided to quit while she was still on top. Fellow number-ones like Novak Djokovic and Roger Federer already counted her as a role model, but as the flood of retirement messages streamed in from all over the world, she realized she had become a hero even outside her game.

Esther used that visibility to keep raising the profile of Paralympic sport. She founded the Esther Vergeer Foundation to create opportunities for children with disabilities to participate in athletics.

She's also passionate about integrating Paralympic and able-bodied competitions. For much of her storied career, when Esther "took home" a trophy, it was literally to her childhood home. The prize money for wheelchair winners was so negligible—sometimes as little as $1,000 per tournament—that she had to live with her parents and seek sponsorships to play full-time. Today, she's ensuring that more disabled athletes get the chance to go pro by being paid to play.

Long known as one of the most decorated athletes in Dutch sports history, Esther was inducted into the International Tennis Hall of Fame in 2023.

BRAIN HEMORRHAGE AND STROKE

The brain needs a constant supply of nutrients and oxygen in order to function. Blood vessels bring these substances to the brain to feed cells that send information through the spinal cord to other parts of the body, allowing for movement. Blood vessels can burst, causing a "brain bleed" or hemorrhage, which results in blood pooling and putting pressure on the brain. Spinal defects can also restrict blood flow to the brain.

A stroke, often referred to as a "brain attack," occurs when blood cannot reach the brain, causing brain cells to die. Once dead, brain cells cannot regenerate, which can make a person's body stop working temporarily, or it can permanently cause physical, mental, and task-specific disabilities. After a stroke, some people may need various forms of therapy to rehabilitate and recover their memory, speech, or movement. Others will change their lifestyles and may need support from caregivers to manage lifelong disabilities such as paralysis.

> " My will to win, my will to be the best I could be is the thing that set me apart from the others. "

ESTHER VERGEER

PETER DINKLAGE

THE ACTOR WHO SAID "NO"

Peter Dinklage wanted to be an actor. But just because he was 4-foot-5, it didn't mean he wanted to appear as an elf or a leprechaun—or a punchline. He struggled for more than a decade to land parts that he could live with—or that paid more than 50 bucks. But in the end, his uncompromising stand paid off. Saying no to typecasting eventually led to some riveting roles, like the one that made him famous in the epic *Game of Thrones*.

NAME: *Peter Hayden Dinklage*

BORN: June 11, 1969

NATIONALITY: American

PROFESSION: Actor

Even when he could not afford to be, even back in the days when he was "paying for dinner at the bodega with dimes," Peter Dinklage was choosy about which parts to take. The actor was born with achondroplasia, a form of dwarfism that affects bone growth. Though he may not be as tall as your average leading man, he didn't want the characters he played to be defined by being little. It made the road to becoming a working actor a lot tougher, but in the long run, the well-rounded roles he was holding out for did turn up—and paved the way for change.

Peter grew up in New Jersey—in a house with no television! His older brother (now a professional violinist and concertmaster) first got him into performing. They started out collaborating on puppet musicals put on for neighbors, and both ended up pursuing performing arts in college.

Peter graduated from Bennington College with a drama degree, ready to chase his dreams. He moved to Brooklyn with a friend where they planned to create their own theater company. When their venture didn't get off the ground, Peter found himself living alone in an apartment without heat and doing data entry to fund his acting.

At age 29, Peter finally decided it was now or never. He quit his day job and committed himself to making a living as an actor. He managed to do it—but only just. And he did it, not by having an agent, but by finding friends who believed in him. Friends like actor-director Steve Buscemi, who gave Peter his movie debut in the dark comedy *Living in Oblivion* (1995) or writer-director Tom McCarthy, who was so taken with Peter's "leading man qualities" in the play *The Killing Act* that he ended up writing an indie film for him to star in. *The Station Agent* (2003) jump-started both of their careers and became a fan favorite of the festival circuit.

Then, in 2011, 20 years after he moved to New York to start his acting career, his relentless hard work finally led to a big break. Still, when his friend, *Game of Thrones* creator David Benioff, first approached Peter to join the show, he was reluctant to say yes. He'd recently donned a long red beard to play Trumpkin in an installment of *The Chronicles of Narnia*, and he wasn't ready to step into the pointy shoes of another fantasy dwarf. David assured him that Tyrion Lannister was not your typical little person, and Peter ensured that the sharp-witted outcast became one of the most compelling characters on television. One of the few members of the ensemble to survive all eight seasons of the gory epic, Tyrion earned Peter four Emmys, a Golden Globe, and the rightful title as one of the highest paid actors on the small screen.

Since then, Peter has enjoyed his choice of parts. He's done voice acting for animated features, played a supervillain in the Marvel X-Men franchise, starred as the romantic hero Cyrano de Bergerac on stage and screen, and got Disney to rethink *Snow White*'s "seven dwarfs." His greatest role? Showing us we all that have the power to reject the status quo.

ACHONDROPLASIA

Individuals with achondroplasia, a form of dwarfism, reach an adult height of 4-foot-10 or below. As children, it may take more time to meet developmental milestones. Due to unique genetic coding that affects a protein in the body called the fibroblast growth factor receptor, cartilage and bones grow at a slower pace, which results in short stature, shortened limbs, and larger skulls.

Some with achondroplasia manage their health with specialists to lead healthy, active lives. While many customize their homes to their height, others prefer to use stools and other tools to maneuver environments built for the nondisabled. There are global organizations for little people that provide support, medical advice, and community.

When speaking to someone with achondroplasia, it's preferable that you use the person's name. If you need to describe someone with achondroplasia, you can ask what language they prefer. Some options include a little person (or LP), a person of short stature, or an individual with dwarfism.

> " Don't bother telling the world you are ready. Show it. Do it.

PETER DINKLAGE

TEMPLE GRANDIN

INVENTOR WHO THINKS IN PICTURES

When Temple Grandin was diagnosed with autism in 1950, doctors recommended that she be institutionalized. Instead, her mother found a way to help her thrive in her own way. Now a leading light for animal welfare and the most famous advocate for people living with autism, Dr. Grandin has an urgent message: We need all of our differently abled brains to solve the world's big problems.

NAME: **Mary Temple Grandin**
BORN: August 29, 1947
NATIONALITY: American
PROFESSION: Animal scientist, industrial designer, educator, and author

When, in 1950 in Boston, doctors told Temple Grandin's parents that she had autism, they were faced with a tough decision and a bunch of unknowns. They knew that their toddler hadn't spoken a word till she was almost four. They knew she had regularly hummed, screamed, and shown repetitive behaviors that could flare up into fierce tantrums. Believing that she would never be able to fit in to the "neurotypical" social world, doctors advised that Temple be sent away to an institution.

At the time, not much was known about autism or how to address its impacts. Still, when Temple's mother Eustacia was told that her daughter could "never" communicate with others or get an education, she found ways to prove naysayers wrong. Eustacia meticulously trained Temple to observe social cues and found a school that would nurture her unique mind. Her mom's grit rubbed off. Temple persevered to have not just an ordinary life, but an extraordinary one.

Today, we know that people on the autism spectrum have brains that work differently from others. Those differences can cause difficulties with social interactions and impact on learning, attention, and movement. But thanks to Temple, we know that different doesn't mean less than. In fact, Temple's logical, visual style of thinking and intense focus on her interests have helped to make her one of the most prominent scholars in her field and one of the most impactful advocates for kids growing up with autism.

Temple describes herself as a "visual thinker." Instead of processing the world through words, she starts from images. This turns out to be a huge asset in her field—animal science—because animals also tend to think with pictures. Like Temple, they're also highly sensitive to touch and sound. Having formed an interest in cattle from visiting her aunt and uncle's ranch, she decided to use her special insight into cow brains to help make the industry more humane. At first, ranchers were skeptical of the "girl nerd" with a PhD in animal husbandry, but now more than half the cattle in the United States are handled in facilities she designed to reduce the livestock's stress and improve their quality of life.

Today, this barrier-breaking scientist's story is well known to the world. A 1993 *New Yorker* profile of her provided one of the earliest first-person accounts of autistic experience, which she memorably described as like being "an anthropologist on Mars." By 2010, she had been named as one of *TIME* magazine's 100 most influential people and had an Emmy-winning movie made about her life. She has written best-selling books, lectured around the world on the need for "neurodiversity," and been inducted into the American Academy of Arts and Sciences.

Recently, a statue of Temple—the first at Colorado State University to honor a woman—was unveiled on the campus, where she continues to be a beloved professor. The bronze sculpture shows her casually sitting on the ground, elbows on knees, in one of her signature embroidered Western shirts, looking off in the distance as if picturing her next big invention.

"

I WANT US COLLECTIVELY,
AS CITIZENS OF THE WORLD,
TO RECLAIM OUR ABILITY TO
CREATE AND INNOVATE IN A
RAPIDLY CHANGING WORLD,
RECOGNIZING WHAT WE GAIN
BY HARNESSING THE POWER
OF EVERY KIND OF MIND.

"

TEMPLE GRANDIN

RJ MITTE

ACTIVIST-ACTOR

RJ Mitte came to Hollywood by chance—
after his little sister was serendipitously
scouted in a Louisiana water park.
But he took the opportunity to bump
elbows with talent agents and ran with
it, searching for roles where he could
make a difference to others with cerebral
palsy. Two years later, he hit the jackpot,
winning a game-changing part in one
of the greatest shows ever to grace the
small screen.

NAME: *Roy Frank "RJ" Mitte III*

BORN: August 21, 1992

NATIONALITY: American

PROFESSION: Actor

RJ Mitte arrived in Hollywood, California, after a Southern upbringing. He was born and adopted as an infant in Jackson, Mississippi. His parents split soon after adopting him. He was raised by his mother, often moving between his grandparents' houses on a Texas ranch and a Louisiana farm.

At age three, RJ was diagnosed with cerebral palsy (CP), a neurological condition that affects movement, balance, and coordination. He wore leg braces and casts to straighten his limbs through much of his childhood and did speech therapy to practice clear communication.

His family—including a former-Marine grandfather who never allowed him to say "can't"— helped him to see his diagnosis as empowering. From a very young age, he was focused on how to improve his body and his mind. It made him strong and compassionate. He needed that strength when his mother was partially paralyzed in a car accident in 2006. She was fired from her job, and at age 13, RJ found himself needing to step up to take care of his family.

RJ's toddler sister had been randomly spotted at a water park by a casting director on vacation. She was offered a role in a movie, and the family decided to relocate to Hollywood so that she could sign with a talent manager. When the agent met RJ, she decided to sign him, too. At first, he thought of acting as a way to make friends in a new place, but he soon realized it was also a golden opportunity to support his family while educating audiences about CP.

He had only worked as an uncredited extra on shows like Disney's *Hannah Montana*, when in 2008, he scored the role of a lifetime. RJ was cast as Walter "Flynn" White, Jr. in *Breaking Bad*—a show so groundbreaking, it actually holds the world record for being the most critically acclaimed television program of all time. Flynn had a more severe case of CP than him. RJ had to learn how to use crutches and alter his speech to play the part. His authentic performance as the unlikely drug kingpin's son—who was in many ways the unwitting hero to his dad's antihero—launched his career. Soon, he was acting in multiple TV shows, producing movies, modeling for an international GAP campaign, and walking the runway for the likes of Vivienne Westwood. He's also gone from small to big screen, starring in movies like the thriller *The Oak Room* (2020) and *Triumph* (2021), a feel-good sports story about a high school kid with CP who beats the odds to become a wrestler.

No matter where his career takes him, he's still dedicated to going home to his mom and sister, and to being a vocal advocate for a more inclusive entertainment industry. As RJ, the Screen Actors Guild's spokesperson for actors with disabilities and an ambassador for United Cerebral Palsy, says: "Representation is everything."

CEREBRAL PALSY

Cerebral palsy (CP) is a condition that influences muscles and movement due to miscommunication between the brain and body. One type of CP causes stiff muscles, while other kinds stimulate involuntary and shaky motions. CP can impact balance and depth perception, as well as other tasks like chewing, swallowing, speaking, breathing, and bladder and bowel regulation.

Many people with CP live independently by simply doing things to accommodate their uniqueness. While others may need support from caregivers and assistive devices to help them communicate and move such as wheelchairs, walkers, and adaptive bicycles. If you have CP, you can build your confidence by focusing on your strengths and connecting with those who share your way of life. If you do not have CP, you can support those who do by getting to know them, including them in activities, and asking if and how they may want assistance. Remember, we are all different and need a number of tools to live our lives in healthy and happy ways!

"
I believe that disabilities are a personal challenge, to an individual to overcome things that most people could not. By doing that, you gain so much knowledge.
"

RJ MITTE

BARBARA JORDAN

TRAILBLAZING POLITICIAN

Barbara Jordan was a true pioneer in US politics. Her array of firsts included being the first African American woman to head a state Senate and the first female keynoter at her party's national convention. She accomplished many of her firsts after being diagnosed with multiple sclerosis. But whether leaning on a cane or assisted by a wheelchair, Barbara continued to use her powerful voice to stand up for what she believed in.

NAME: *Barbara Charline Jordan*

BORN: **February 21, 1936**   DIED: **January 17, 1996** (age 59)

NATIONALITY: **American**

PROFESSION: **Lawyer, educator, and politician**

Barbara Jordan grew up in a Houston, Texas, household with two parents who were gifted public speakers.

After graduating with a law degree from Boston University in 1960, she returned to Houston to practice, serving as an administrative assistant to a county judge while running campaigns to get people out to vote in predominantly African American districts. Two years later, she ran for office herself. Barbara twice lost her bid to join the Texas House of Representatives before being elected to the state's Senate instead.

In 1966, she was the first African American woman to hold that office—and to be elected to the US Senate period since 1883. At first, she received a frosty reception from the 30 other (white, male) senators, but she immediately impressed with her practical and cooperative leadership. Just six years later, those same officials picked her to be president of the Senate, with nominations from both sides of the aisle.

That same year, Barbara won a seat in the US Congress as a Democratic Representative from Texas. The first African American congressperson to be elected from a Southern state in the twentieth century, she served three landmark terms, raking in a staggering 85 percent of the vote in her two re-election campaigns.

Even though she was new to Washington, DC, Barbara used her savvy as a negotiator to get herself a seat at the table on the powerful House Judiciary Committee. In 1973, her forceful opening remarks to the impeachment proceedings that would prompt President Richard Nixon to resign gained her a national following. "I am not going to sit here," she said, "and be an idle spectator to the diminution, the subversion, the destruction of the Constitution." If her fellow committee members failed to convict Nixon, she calmly suggested, "then perhaps the eighteenth-century Constitution should be abandoned to a twentieth-century paper shredder." Admiring calls, letters, and editorials streamed in—someone even put up a "thank you" billboard!

Just as Barbara was beginning to soar in national politics, she was diagnosed with multiple sclerosis (MS). MS is a lifelong condition that impairs the central nervous system. She didn't go public with the diagnosis, but she began using a cane to help her walk and required a personal assistant to help her remain fully functional. Still, she stuck to her longtime agenda, backing laws that expanded civil and voting rights, protecting against discrimination, and supporting blue-collar workers.

In 1976, Barbara became the first African American and first woman keynote speaker at the Democratic National Convention, firing up the crowd with her famous speech about diversity and inclusivity, "All Together Now." She retired from Congress in 1979 to become a chaired professor of public policy at the University of Texas.

In 1992, Barbara reprised her keynote at the DNC, this time in a wheelchair. The audience erupted in applause as she called on leaders to make good on the American dream and declared it was high time to nominate a "Madame President." Barbara passed away in 1996 from a complication of leukemia. Even in death, she blazed a trail, becoming the first African American to be buried in the Texas State Cemetery.

> One thing is clear to me: We, as human beings, must be willing to accept people who are different from ourselves.
>
> BARBARA JORDAN

MULTIPLE SCLEROSIS

Multiple sclerosis, or MS, affects a person's central nervous system (CNS). The CNS includes the brain, spinal cord, and a vast network of nerves that carry messages to and from the rest of the body. These messages enable someone to think, feel, speak, and move. MS damages the protective covering of the nerves (known as "myelin"), causing scarring around the nerves, which can interfere with the brain and spinal cord's ability to communicate with the body. People with MS are impacted by the condition differently, depending on the location of the damaged nerves within the brain and spinal cord.

Some individuals with MS may experience weakness, tingling, or numbness in their hands or feet; mood shifts, pain, tiredness, visual issues, difficulty walking, and/or problems with memory. These symptoms can be temporary or permanent, and they may begin as mild, then become more significant as a person ages. Initially, most people with MS experience flare-ups and remissions of their symptoms. Although research is being done to learn more about this condition, a cure has yet to be found. So, people with MS may need medicine, therapy, caregivers, and support from loved ones to manage their condition.

STEPHEN HAWKING

THE SHOOTING STAR OF A SCIENTIST

Born on the three-hundredth anniversary of the death of Galileo, Stephen Hawking seemed destined to enter the annals of astronomy, too. There was just one problem. He was diagnosed with Lou Gehrig's disease while still a student. Rapidly losing control of his body's movements, Stephen surpassed all expectations just by finishing his PhD. He would go on to blow minds with his renowned decades-long career that forever changed our view of the cosmos.

NAME: *Stephen William Hawking*

BORN: January 8, 1942   **DIED:** March 14, 2018 (age 76)

NATIONALITY: British

PROFESSION: Theoretical physicist

Stephen Hawking was not such a remarkable student growing up in England. His parents were both Oxford University grads, but it seemed unlikely that he would secure a place there, until a near-perfect score on his physics evaluation exam earned him a coveted scholarship. He had moved on to a doctoral program in cosmology at Cambridge University, when at 21, his life went supernova.

Stephen was diagnosed with amyotrophic lateral sclerosis (ALS), often known as motor neuron or Lou Gehrig's disease. ALS is uncurable. It's a condition that affects brain and spine function, causing people to increasingly lose control over their movements. Doctors predicted he only had a few years to live. While Stephen's immediate reaction was shock and hopelessness, his roommate at the hospital—a boy suffering with leukemia—made him realize that even he had it better than some. A romance with his soon to be wife and mother of his children also gave him "a reason to live." Determined to make the most of the time he had left, he plunged into what ended up being an amazing five-decade career as a star of theoretical physics.

Known for his groundbreaking work on those most mysterious of space phenomena, black holes, Stephen proposed a novel way to bring together the "vast" and the "tiny" approaches to theoretical physics—general relativity and quantum mechanics. He was named the Lucasian Professor of Mathematics at Cambridge in 1979—a title so prestigious, it was once held by physics great Sir Isaac Newton! One of the youngest members of the Royal Society, Stephen was recognized with a slew of awards, including the America's highest honor, the Presidential Medal of Freedom.

One of the few scientists to become a pop culture phenom, his international best-selling book, *A Brief History of Time*, brought his enormous curiosity, wonder, and insight about the beginnings and end of the universe to a general audience. Known for his sense of humor, he also made cameos on sitcoms like *The Simpsons* and *The Big Bang Theory* and even appeared as a hologram of himself on the sci-fi favorite, *Star Trek*. Eddie Redmayne won an Oscar for playing him in the 2014 biopic, *The Theory of Everything*. When, in 2017, Cambridge decided to provide free access to Stephen's 1965 PhD thesis, their servers immediately crashed from the demand.

As the physicist's fame grew, his mobility decreased. Soon after his diagnosis, Stephen was confined to a wheelchair—a dead giveaway, he joked, to celebrity spotters. In time, he also lost his ability to eat and speak. Tech allowed him to communicate with a speech-generating device that had a menu of words he selected by pointing and later, by moving a cheek muscle.

When he died at 76, droves came out to pay their respects to one of the finest minds and most inspiring survivors of his generation. He was interred in England's national shrine, Westminster Abbey, alongside royalty and scientific giants such as Charles Darwin. To mark his death, the European Space Agency beamed one of his messages of peace and hope toward our nearest black hole by satellite. His extraordinary voice will reach its final destination in 3,500 years.

> I am very aware of the preciousness of time. Seize the moment. Act now.

STEPHEN HAWKING

AMYOTROPHIC LATERAL SCLEROSIS

Amyotrophic lateral sclerosis, or ALS, is also named Lou Gehrig's disease after a New York Yankees baseball player who was diagnosed with the condition in the 1930s. ALS damages motor neurons, causing them to shrink and die. Motor neurons are nerve cells that travel from the brain to the muscles to promote movements like walking, talking, breathing, and jumping.

With damaged motor neurons, muscles become smaller and weaker. People with ALS may twitch or shake, trip or fall, drop items, and speak differently. The condition can worsen over time, making eating, swallowing, and breathing more challenging. Eventually, the body will become paralyzed. However, people with ALS are able to utilize their senses of smell, touch, taste, sight, and sound because sensory neurons remain unaffected.

ALS treatment includes therapy, medicines, and assistive devices like power wheelchairs to help with movement or ventilators to assist with breathing. Many will need the support of a professional caregiver and loved ones. If you know someone with ALS, be patient as you learn their unique communication style and life pace.

MILLIE BOBBY BROWN

UNSTOPPABLE ACTOR

When Millie Bobby Brown wants to do
something, she doesn't let anything stop her.
So why would having hearing loss keep her
from pursuing a career in acting and singing?
Millie turned her loss into an asset that
helped her soar to fame before she
even hit her teens.

NAME: *Millie Bobby Brown*
BORN: February 19, 2004
NATIONALITY: British
PROFESSION: Actor

Millie Bobby Brown had already decided at the age of eight that she was going to be an actor. As it turned out, talent scouts agreed. They convinced her parents to take her to Hollywood where every agent she met with wanted to sign her. She was quickly cast in guest spots on a variety of network TV shows—from the fan-favorite medical drama *Grey's Anatomy* to the Emmy-winning comedy series *Modern Family*. Then, at age 12, the determined kid landed her breakout role as the young hero at the center of the TV sci-fi hit *Stranger Things*.

The precocious Millie was born in Spain to British parents and grew up in England and Orlando, Florida. She had partial hearing loss in one ear, and many rounds of ear tube surgeries failed to solve the problem. Eventually, she became entirely deaf on one side. It might sound like it's a disadvantage for someone whose job profile includes acting and singing to be unable to hear herself, but Millie has turned it into an advantage.

For one, it has made her less self-conscious. Her confidence, firm trust in her instincts, and total commitment to whatever she's doing have set her apart as an actor. As it turned out, only having partial hearing didn't hurt either when it came to electrifying fans and critics in her first major role. *Stranger Things'* Eleven—a girl with psychic superpowers who escapes from a lab where she's being held as a test subject—was not a big talker. Millie talked with her whole face instead, and it earned her the Saturn Award for the Best Performance by a Younger Actor in a Television Series.

Her philosophy—"If you genuinely enjoy doing it, then do it"—has led her to do more things in her first two decades than most people do in a lifetime. Millie had become a producer and modeled for Calvin Klein by age 13, founded her own vegan beauty brand (Florence by Mills) at 15, and published her first novel at 19. Called *Nineteen Steps*, it's a historical thriller based on her own grandma's experience of surviving London air raids during World War II!

Millie's also gotten to play Sherlock Holmes' (equally super-sleuth) sister Enola and faced off against Godzilla on the silver screen. She's been nominated for multiple Emmys and Screen Actors Guild awards. On World Children's Day in 2018, she was appointed as the youngest-ever UNICEF Goodwill Ambassador, joining the likes of David Beckham and Priyanka Chopra to become a global champion of kids' rights. She's even signed up for a Purdue University program to study health and human services with all her free time! It's no wonder that this unstoppable renaissance girl was the youngest person in history to be named among *TIME* magazine's 100 most influential people.

"ONCE I FIND SOMETHING I WANT TO DO, NOBODY'S STOPPING ME."

MILLIE BOBBY BROWN

MICHAEL J. FOX

THE IDOL TURNED ICON

Michael J. Fox was top of the list
of "80s famous." He had already won
three Outstanding Lead Actor Emmys for
the TV show *Family Ties* and headlined
one of the highest-grossing movies of the
decade in *Back to the Future* when, at age
29, he was diagnosed with Parkinson's.
Michael took a temporary step back
from showbiz, but his best act was yet to
come—as the optimistic figurehead for
a community in search of a cure.

NAME: **Michael Andrew Fox**

BORN: June 9, 1961

NATIONALITY: Canadian-American

PROFESSION: Actor and activist

As soon as he turned 18, Michael Andrew Fox left his native Canada to chase his acting dreams in Hollywood. He arrived to find that another actor was already going by "Michael Fox," so he added the distinctive "J." to make his name stand out.

Michael had made his on-screen debut at 15 on a Canadian TV show, but he had to hustle to get work in Hollywood. He found himself selling off personal possessions—from paperback books to pieces of his sectional couch—for grocery money. When he got the call that would change his life, he had to field it in a booth outside a nearby fast-food restaurant because he didn't have a phone. That 1982 call offered him the role of Alex P. Keaton in the show *Family Ties*. The endearing comedy was a perfect fit for the rising star, and soon he was a go-to leading man.

A series of top billings in films like *Teen Wolf*, *High School U.S.A.*, and *The Secret of My Success* made Michael a teen idol of the 1980s. His starring role as Marty McFly in the madcap time-travel movies of *Back to the Future* made him an instant classic. Then, on the set of the 1991 film *Doc Hollywood*, he began to notice a twitch in his finger. Doctors confirmed that it was an early sign of Parkinson's disease (PD).

Michael was only 29 years old. Recently married and a new father, he was just starting a family and at the peak of his success. Doctors told him that he might be able to mask his symptoms and work for another 10 years, but there was no stopping the degenerative condition. Michael would one day lose control over his body movements and coordination—how soon was anybody's guess.

The risk-taking kid, the one who had taken his own destiny into his hands by hocking his guitar to come to Hollywood, found it difficult to cope with his inescapable diagnosis. He was worried that audiences wouldn't be able to laugh at his comedies if they knew he was struggling. So, Michael hid his PD. Weighed down by denial and depression, he began drinking too much alcohol.

Michael's family helped him get sober and accept his condition. He was fronting another Emmy-winning hit series in *Spin City* when, in 1998, he knew it was finally time to go public. As soon as he did, support flooded in. He realized he was part of a community. And he saw for the first time how his past successes and his current situation gave him the "profound opportunity and responsibility" to make a difference. So, in 2000, Michael announced he was stepping back from acting to establish the Michael J. Fox Foundation. The organization has already funded more than $1.5 billion in PD research and is driving the search for a cure.

Today, the actor-activist has become a best-selling author with four books that share his hard-earned optimism. He's also gone back to acting, but he doesn't bother to hide his tremors. In 2023, Michael, the Grammy and four-time Golden Globe winner, was honored with his first Oscar—the Jean Hersholt Humanitarian Award.

> "
> My optimism is fueled by my gratitude.
> And with gratitude, optimism is sustainable.
> "
>
> MICHAEL J. FOX

PARKINSON'S

Parkinson's damages nerve cells in the brain called basal ganglia, which communicate with the body about movement. This impacts a person's ability to manage their mobility, memory, behavior, and emotions. People with Parkinson's may experience trembling in their hands, stiffness in their bodies, and difficulties with thinking and memory. Standing, balance, coordination, and walking also may be challenging. These symptoms usually develop slowly over long periods of time.

Scientists are hopeful that a cure will be discovered soon. Until then, people with Parkinson's take medicine, receive therapy treatments, or have surgeries that can improve or even eliminate symptoms. Adjustments to their lifestyle and assistive devices can help individuals with Parkinson's manage daily activities such as walking, eating, getting dressed, writing, and texting. If you have Parkinson's, you can ask those around you for the help you need to succeed. If you don't, you can be generous in helping those who do ask for it!

WARWICK DAVIS

THE WORLD'S SHORTEST LEADING ACTOR

The odds of getting the rare bone growth condition spondyloepiphyseal dysplasia congenita are just one in 3.4 million. The odds of having a career like Warwick Davis are even slimmer. Warwick took the rare opportunity of being an extra in his favorite film series and rolled it into a lifelong vocation that has seen him play an Ewok, goblin, wizard, and his own hilarious self. Recently, he even treated fans to a reprise of his most famous role: the aspiring sorcerer Willow Ufgood.

NAME: **Warwick Davis**

BORN: **February 3, 1970**

NATIONALITY: **British**

PROFESSION: **Actor**

When Warwick Davis' grandmother heard a commercial calling for people under four feet tall to join the cast of *Return of the Jedi*, she knew her 11-year-old grandson would be interested. At 2-foot-11, Warwick more than fit the bill. He was also a diehard *Star Wars* fan.

Warwick eagerly attended the audition and was signed as an Ewok extra. But when the actor playing the lead Ewok Wicket got sick, creator George Lucas handpicked Warwick to take over the iconic role. Warwick came away from the dream experience with a complete set of *Star Wars* action figures (courtesy of Luke Skywalker himself, Mark Hamill) and an unexpected acting career.

Born with spondyloepiphyseal dysplasia congenita (SEDc), a rare inherited condition that affects bone growth, Warwick never grew taller than 3-foot-6. Still, the English actor has found plenty of ways to make his height a major draw and important talking point. In fact, his epic debut in a galaxy far, far away was so memorable that it inspired George Lucas and acclaimed director Ron Howard to produce a fantasy adventure film specifically for Warwick—1988's *Willow*. Starring as the title character alongside Hollywood heartthrob Val Kilmer, Warwick finally got to show his face to fans. His performance cast a spell over audiences—including the Prince and Princess of Wales who granted the movie a Royal Premiere.

Since then, he's featured in some of the greatest cult classics of all time—from *Labyrinth* (with rock legend David Bowie!) to the horror flick *Leprechaun* and its FIVE gruesome-funny sequels. He's also been in some heavy-hitting blockbusters, including eight *Star Wars* movies (playing 15 characters) and all eight *Harry Potter* films as Professor Flitwick and the Goblin Griphook. The versatile actor can do serious dramas, too, such as embodying the jazz performer Oberon in the Oscar-winning biopic based on the life of Ray Charles. The movies he's been in have brought in more than $14 billion at the box office, making him one of the top 20 highest-grossing actors in the world.

Never one to sidestep discussions of his size, Warwick has produced many projects that speak to the experience of those with dwarfism, including a TV series cowritten with comedian Ricky Gervais: *Life's Too Short*.

While he's famous for approaching his (SEDc) with humor, living with it has often been tough. It's led to childhood surgeries and multiple health issues like dislocated hips and arthritis, plus the heartbreaking loss of his first two children with wife Samantha. But Warwick has used his high-profile position to create opportunities for others within the community.

He cofounded a nonprofit, Little People UK, to support people with dwarfism. He established the Reduced Height Theatre Company to stage productions cast entirely with short actors on scaled-down sets. And he's codirector of "the biggest agency for short actors"—named Willow Management after the film that officially made him the world's shortest leading man.

SPONDYLOEPIPHYSEAL DYSPLASIA CONGENITA

Spondyloepiphyseal dysplasia congenita (SEDc), a form of dwarfism, is present at birth. The condition results in lower stature due to the shortened length of the spine, arms, and legs, but it can also cause vision and hearing challenges. The feet, hands, and heads of those with SEDc remain standard sizes.

The condition impacts each person differently, so treatment programs will be unique for every individual. They may include bracing various parts of the body to aid in stability, assistive devices to improve hearing and vision, medication, therapies, and surgeries. Environments designed for the non-disabled can be adapted to the height of those with SEDc, so that they can navigate their surroundings independently.

Individuals with SEDc can live long, healthy lives and should always be treated according to their age, not their size. We can all respect and include each other regardless of appearance or height differences, and we can work together to improve our homes, schools, recreational parks, and workplaces, so that they are suitable for everyone.

"

My parents armed me with an amazing sense of humor, and it's what you need when, well, it's what anyone needs in this world.

"

WARWICK DAVIS

NICK VUJICIC

ROLE MODEL
WITHOUT LIMITS

Surfing and skydiving videos are pretty standard fare on YouTube . . . not so much when the person hitting the waves or free falling has no limbs. Born without arms or legs, Nick Vujicic has made an art out of completely ignoring his supposed limitations. Powered by his faith, Nick has dedicated his life to empowering others to act on their limitless potential.

NAME: **Nick James Vujicic**

BORN: December 4, 1982

NATIONALITY: **Australian-American**

PROFESSION: **Motivational speaker**

Nick Vujicic was born in Australia to parents who were devout Serbian Orthodox immigrants from Yugoslavia. Though otherwise healthy, baby Nicholas had a rare genetic condition called tetra-amelia syndrome that left him with no arms or legs—just two small, atypical feet. His parents were so shocked and overwhelmed by their firstborn child's disability that it took them months even to be able to hold him. But their strong faith helped them accept their son as a gift who was part of God's plan. As Nick found ways to stand and walk around like any infant, their grief at his limitations soon gave way to amazement at his abilities. That amazement has only grown.

While Nick was playful and determined from the start, he went through a rough patch after he started school. Bullied and depressed about his differences, he often thought about taking his own life at only 10 years old. Not wanting to upset his family kept him from the brink, and eventually they helped restore his irrepressible zeal for life. He learned to play football and skateboard. He hitched rides on friends' bicycle handlebars. He ran for student body president at his elementary school and won—his first official public speaking gig.

Inspired by his Christian faith, Nick soon graduated from speaking to schoolmates to speaking to church groups. His story and stage presence were so electrifying that his audiences have kept expanding exponentially ever since. Today, Nick has addressed some of the biggest arenas around. He's presented at the World Economic Forum and met six presidents. He's given a Lifeclass with Oprah and reached tens of millions of people online. He's also used his clout as a keynoter to create the nonprofit ministry Life Without Limbs; he's worked with governments on anti-bullying campaigns and designed a special curriculum for schoolkids called "Attitude Is Altitude." An author of eight titles and counting, Nick's first book *Life Without Limits: Inspiration for a Ridiculously Good Life* has been translated into 32 languages.

Nick inspires others by practicing what he preaches, overcoming obstacles to thrive. When Nick was a kid, surgeons operated on the larger foot attached to his left hip, which he affectionately refers to as his "chicken drumstick." The surgery separated his fused-together toes, which now double as fingers for Nick. He uses them to do things like hold on to objects, flip pages, operate phones, type on his computer (at 43 words per minute!), and drive an electric wheelchair.

Always kind of a daredevil, Nick has done plenty of things that defy expectations. The videos he's shared of him doing backflips on a trampoline, skydiving, snowboarding, or surfing invite people to rethink their own potential. But some of the most moving videos (viewed millions of times) are of much more ordinary moments, like Nick joyfully playing a game of hide-and-seek with his toddler son—something his parents never imagined was possible. Nick clearly did, and that has made all the difference.

> If you can't get a miracle, become one.

NICK VUJICIC

TETRA-AMELIA SYNDROME

Tetra-amelia syndrome, or TETAMS, is characterized by the absence of all four limbs—both arms and legs. However, it can also impact other areas of the body as well. The condition occurs while the fetus is developing during pregnancy and is sometimes diagnosed through ultrasounds. Many babies who have TETAMS do not live past birth due to medical complications. So those who do can be celebrated for the survivors they are!

The absence of limbs does not mean the inability to live a fulfilling life. People with TETAMS will need support from caregivers for many of their daily activities, and they must use assistive devices like wheelchairs that can be operated by the head, chin, or tongue. With the right support, they can pursue their passions and fulfill their dreams! No matter what our bodies look like, we can all help each other to live our best lives.

ALI STROKER

THEATER HISTORYMAKER

Ali Stroker had never seen someone on Broadway using a wheelchair except as a prop. That didn't stop the budding musical theater star from dreaming about making it to the big time. She became not only the first wheelchair user to appear in a Broadway show but also the first to win a Tony Award. With her impressive range of artistic projects, Ali is showing that her wheelchair is more than a way to get around. It's also a catalyst for creativity.

NAME: **Alyson Mackenzie "Ali" Stroker**

BORN: June 16, 1987

NATIONALITY: American

PROFESSION: Actress, author, singer

When Ali Stroker entered stage left for Deaf West Theatre's 2015 production of the musical *Spring Awakening*, she wheeled her way into history. She became the first actor who uses a wheelchair for mobility to appear in a Broadway show. When, three years later, she was cast as Ado Annie for a daring modern revival of the Rogers and Hammerstein classic *Oklahoma!*, she had no idea the role would land her back on Broadway. But, the initial run was so good and breathtakingly original that it was tapped to move to the world's most famous theater district.

Ado Annie is a comic role usually played as a one-dimensional caricature, but Ali's portrayal made her powerfully real. The performance saw her nominated for the theater industry's top honor, a Tony Award. When she was named Best Featured Actress, she couldn't walk down the aisle and go up the steps to receive her trophy. Instead, she had to gain access to the stage via an alternative backstage route. It was one small example of the many accessibility issues Ali had to face on her journey to becoming the first wheelchair user to take home a Tony. "This award," she said in her acceptance speech, "is for every kid who is watching tonight who has a disability, who has a limitation, who has a challenge, who has been waiting to see themselves represented in this arena. *You are.*"

Ali was only two years old when a car accident left her paralyzed from the waist down. She quickly adjusted to her new reality in a wheelchair, and then at age seven, she discovered something that made her feel like she was soaring: musical theater. Soon, Ali was nabbing leading roles in community productions, like the title character in *Annie* and Dorothy in *The Wizard of Oz*. Being entrusted to play such beloved parts gave Ali the self-confidence she needed to be a wheelchair trailblazer in the arts world.

After becoming the first wheelchair user to earn a drama degree at NYU's Tisch School of Arts, Ali got her professional start in 2012 by auditioning for a reality TV competition. Squaring off against other amazing triple-threats (singer-dancer-actors) on *The Glee Project*, she won a guest-starring role on the hit high-school dramedy *Glee*. Her scene-stealing stint as Miss Pillsbury's delightfully snide niece set Ali up for multiple other TV guest spots on everything from *Charmed* to *Blue Bloods* to *Ozark*.

When she's not gracing stage or screen, she's performing her cabaret act at some of the United States' fanciest venues, like New York's Carnegie Hall. She's also tried her hand at fiction, coauthoring two kids' novels that star Nat Beacon, a young theater lover who has a lot in common with her fabulous creator. Through all her work and advocacy, Ali is pushing to see more characters with disabilities in the spotlight— after all, a quarter of people in the United States have one. And yet, she doesn't want them to be limited to "inspirational" stories. She'd rather see complex, compelling characters where "we don't assume disability rules their lives"—roles, that is, like the ones Ali has chosen to play.

"
REPRESENTATION CAN CHANGE SOMEONE'S MIND. I CAN BE A REMINDER OF THE STRENGTH AND COURAGE ALREADY INSIDE OF THEM.

"

ALI STROKER

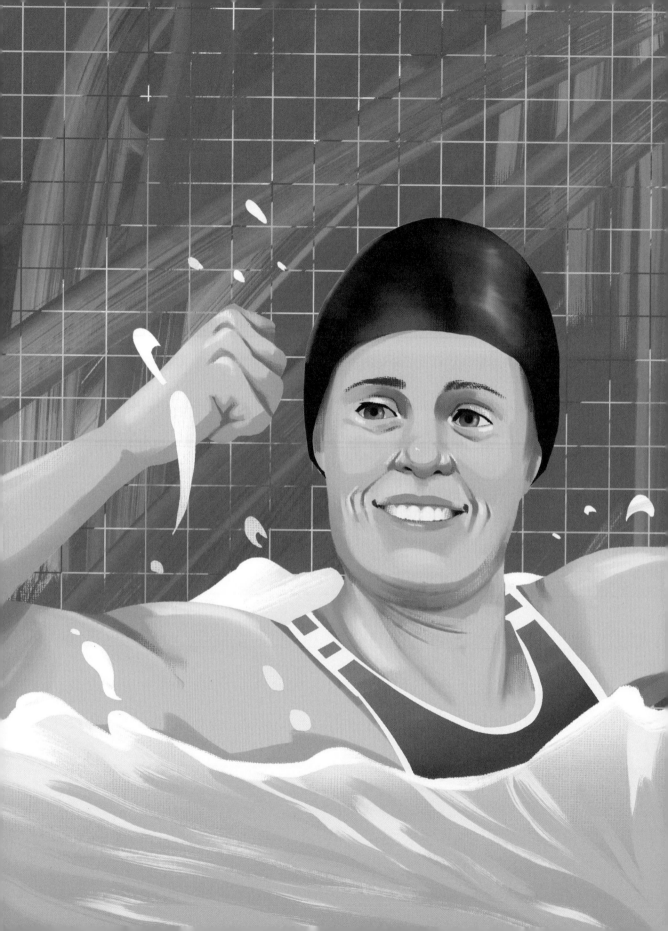

TRISCHA ZORN

The most successful Paralympian of all time, Trischa Zorn won her last of 55 medals 24 years after her first. In the process, she set eight world records and earned two degrees. Between her seven trips to the Paralympic Games, the blind swimmer moonlighted as an educator for students with disabilities, encouraging them to set epic goals for themselves.

NAME: *Trischa Zorn*

BORN: June 1, 1964

NATIONALITY: American

PROFESSION: Swimmer and attorney

Trischa Zorn was born with a genetic condition called aniridia that left her legally blind. It meant that her irises didn't develop to adjust to different levels of light, making the center of her eyes look entirely black instead of having a circle of color.

Trischa grew up in Southern California. She found school challenging at first. The limited resources available for special education in the 1970s made learning very difficult. Her most enduring early lessons came through her love of swimming. Trischa trained with the elite Mission Viejo Nadadores Swim Team from the age of 10 where the coaches gave her the recipe for her future success: the "3 Ds" (discipline, dedication, determination)—AND time management.

In 1980, at the age of 16, Trischa put that recipe into action. She tried out for the U.S. National Team that was headed to the Moscow Summer Olympics in her best event (backstroke), losing out on a spot by mere fractions of a second. That same year, she made her Paralympics debut, winning a stunning seven gold medals.

She also swam competitively in college. Recruited by the University of Nebraska, Trischa became the first visually impaired athlete to earn a full, top-tier athletic scholarship. With better learning support, she thrived as a student. She earned a top degree in special education and came away as a four-time All-American, both in backstroke and academics. In between Games, Trischa became the teacher she'd always wanted to have. Working in classrooms with disabled students in inner-city Indianapolis, the super-athlete was an energizing role model for her students.

Her crazy-fast speeds (she still holds two Paralympic world records—in backstroke and medley) made some people doubt her disability. Her Paralympic classification was even formally challenged (and upheld) at the 2000 Games in Sydney, where she went on to win five medals. Three years later, Trischa signed up to be one of the first patients with aniridia to trial a new technology. A renowned surgeon inserted artificial irises into her eyes, which didn't restore her sight completely but improved it to 20/850 (having 20/200 vision qualifies someone as legally blind).

While Trischa ended up topping the podium 41 times, she's most proud of her last of 55 medals, a bronze that she won at her seventh and final Games. She was 40 years old and had been spending most of her time attending law school since the last Paralympics. Then, Trischa's super-supportive mother died from cancer while she was training for the competition. Feeling the devastating absence of her number one fan, Trischa didn't place in three events. But she rallied to take third in the 100-meter backstroke, a touching tribute to her beloved mom.

Trischa retired from swimming as the most decorated Paralympic athlete in history—a record that's not likely to be broken. Today, the 2022 inductee into the U.S. Olympic & Paralympic Hall of Fame is a practicing attorney who works for the U.S. Department of Veterans Affairs. She still hits the pool regularly, but now it's just for fun—or to mentor the next great Paralympian.

Once you are at the top of the mountain, it is awesome. But staying on top of that mountain is harder than the original climb.

TRISCHA ZORN

ANIRIDIA

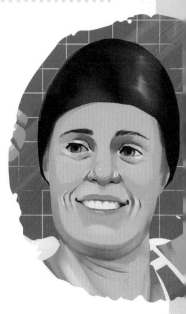

Individuals are diagnosed with aniridia when the colorful part of the eye, called the iris, is incomplete or missing. Without the iris, the pupil—or the round opening in the center of the eye—may be shaped differently or enlarged. This can impact the sharpness of someone's vision and cause sensitivity to light or involuntary eye movements. These symptoms may be present at birth, while others may occur as the individual ages. People with aniridia may also experience other eye conditions that can result in partial or complete vision loss.

Some people with aniridia will wear special glasses that protect the eye, while others may choose to place painted contact lenses into their eyes to add the appearance of a colorful iris. Diversity of appearance makes life fun and interesting. So no matter what your eye color is (or lack thereof), let's celebrate the attributes that make each of us unique!

AARON FOTHERINGHAM

EXTREME ATHLETE

If a sport you want to do doesn't exist, why not invent it? That's what Aaron Fotheringham has done, as the first WCMX (wheelchair motocross) rider in history. Aaron has wowed crowds with his inventive takes on BMX tricks, from a midair 180 to a double backflip 360. While he mulls over his design for "the most wicked chair in the world," he's also become a coach for the next gen of extreme wheelchair athletes.

NAME: **_Aaron "Wheelz" Fotheringham_**

BORN: **November 8, 1991**

NATIONALITY: **American**

PROFESSION: **WCMX rider**

The first time Aaron Fotheringham dropped in a four-foot quarter-pipe, he fell down. Hard. But he got up to try again—and again and again—until he got the ride right, and then he was hooked.

Aaron grew up in Las Vegas, Nevada. The third of six adopted children in his family, he was born with spina bifida, a spinal cord defect, which left him without the use of his legs. That didn't mean he ever sat still for long. As a toddler, he put on a Superman cape and "flew" around the house on crutches. He also loved following his older brother Brian to the local skate park to watch him pull BMX stunts. Then one day, Brian encouraged him to give his own wheels a whirl, and his parents gave him the thumbs up to try.

Soon, Aaron was finding ways to nail the moves his friends were doing on their bikes. In other sports he'd tried, he was put in "adaptive" settings. With BMX, he could just hang out in the skate park with his peers, swapping stunts. By the time he was a teen, only his mom called him Aaron anymore. Everyone else knew him as the daredevil "Wheelz." He challenged himself to enter competitions—and even won a few, like the Vegas AmJam BMX Finals—but his biggest drive was always just to up his own game. In the process, he ended up pioneering a new sport: wheelchair motocross, or WCMX.

Almost every move Wheelz mastered became a history-making first. In 2006, at age 14, he landed the first wheelchair backflip. In 2010, he did the first ever double and in 2011, the first ever front flip. He secured a double entry in the _Guinness World Records_ during one run in 2018—the longest wheelchair ramp jump (70-feet) and the highest wheelchair hand plant (27-feet-6.7 inches).

With each new trick Wheelz landed in front of cheering audiences or posted online, his global following grew. He's rolled in the X Games and toured the world with Nitro Circus, performing the gnarliest of live stunts for packed stadiums of extreme sports fans. In 2022, he introduced the Nitro Circus' infamous Giganta Ramp to TV audiences by competing on _America's Got Talent Extreme_. Aaron's moves were also showcased to museum-going audiences with an installation that featured one of his specially designed chairs in the Smithsonian National Museum of American History in Washington, DC. The WCMX founder commemorated the occasion with the hashtag #onesmallpushforwheelkind.

While most of Wheelz's tricks fall into the "do not try this at home" category, his boundary-pushing courage inspires people well beyond the half-pipe. He's also been a model for giving back to his community from the start, coaching and mentoring kids with disabilities while giving them living proof that a wheelchair can be "a tool, not a restriction."

> "There is something magical about thinking you're absolutely gonna die but then sticking the landing.

AARON FOTHERINGHAM

SPINA BIFIDA

Infants have spina bifida when their spines develop with an opening between the bones. Sometimes the meninges (the layers of membranes that protect the spinal cord), the sac that holds spinal fluid, and/or the spinal cord—push through this opening and protrude through the skin in the back.

Depending on the type and severity of the condition, some children will have few or no symptoms, while others may experience weakness, a lack of bladder control, or paralysis. Treatment of spina bifida varies. For those who need surgery, sometimes it can be done while the fetus is still in the womb!

Many with spina bifida can lead independent lives with little support, while others will need assistance to manage their condition for life. If you have spina bifida, you can receive resources from organizations focused on the condition. If you do not, you can support those who do by learning more about it and asking how you can help!

AMY PURDY

ACTION SPORTS HERO

Amy Purdy came back from a death-defying encounter with meningitis to become the most decorated Paralympic snowboarder in US history. Since then, the double amputee has gone from snowboard cross star to top motivational speaker who counts Madonna and Oprah among her fans. Also a model, actor, clothing designer, nonprofit founder, TV personality, spokesperson, and author, Amy's experience with "adaptive" living has sparked an inspired life.

NAME: **Amelia Michelle "Amy" Purdy**

BORN: **November 7, 1979**

NATIONALITY: **American**

PROFESSION: **Para snowboarder**

One day, massage therapist Amy Purdy felt a bit under the weather. The next day, she was being rushed to the hospital as her organs shut down, one by one. As it turned out, she had a very dangerous strain of bacterial meningitis. Doctors gave her a 2 percent chance of surviving the rare blood infection. She was only 19.

Amy beat the odds, with the help of blood transfusions, surgery to remove her ruptured spleen, an induced coma, and an organ transplant (with a kidney, courtesy of her father). However, the septic shock her body experienced—a state in which a person's blood pressure is so low due to infection that the blood does not reach their limbs and vital organs—forced doctors to amputate her legs below the knees.

Amy came away from the ordeal with a new lease on life. She had begun snowboarding at age 15, and suddenly she knew she had to get back to the slopes. There weren't any prosthetic limbs or feet that fit into her board, so she worked with a doctor to make some, often keeping her inventions together with rusty bolts and neon duct tape. Just three months after her life-saving kidney transplant, she signed up to compete in the USASA National Snowboarding Championship. She carved her way to a miraculous three medals.

From then on, Amy became an action sports icon. The most decorated Paralympic snowboarder in US history, she is responsible for getting her sport onto the roster at the Paralympic Winter Games. Besides pulling off a three-peat of World Cup gold medals in snowboard cross, Amy has recruited and trained some of her finest competitors. In 2005, she cofounded Adaptive Action Sports to get more of the disabled community on a board.

The self-styled "fembot" has also found her way into broader popular culture. She's modeled, starred in a Madonna music video, acted in an award-winning indie film, and won the hearts of audiences in TWO reality TV competitions. She and her now-husband appeared on *The Amazing Race* in 2012, and she became the first double-amputee to participate in *Dancing with the Stars* in 2014, finishing in second place!

Today, the "partially bionic" woman has a leg collection to rival her enviable shoe collection. She has at times faced health setbacks that have limited her ability to walk, but all in all, she believes that her new legs have been more enabling than disabling. By approaching her life-changing condition with fun and imagination, Amy has become an in-demand motivational speaker on self-acceptance. Oprah has even named Amy as one of her Top 100 thought leaders. With her best-selling autobiography *On My Own Two Feet* and podcast *Bouncing Forward*, this remarkable athlete is helping others to #LiveInspired.

AMPUTATION

Some people are born with limb differences, while others, due to trauma or other medical conditions, will need to have a part of their body amputated. When a person loses a limb, they may feel sad and frustrated as they learn to adjust to a new way of life without their arm, leg, or both. Many will require emotional and physical support as they heal, practice coordination and balance, as well as learn how to regain function and mobility with prosthetics or other assistive technologies.

If you know someone who has recently lost a limb to amputation, be sure to ask them how they are doing, as well as about ways you can support them. For those who have experienced an amputation, lean into your community for emotional and social support by connecting with others who understand what you are going through. We can all learn and grow from honoring each other's differences and providing safe spaces to speak openly about the challenges and transitions of our lives.

> " True inclusion is being able to represent our unique differences without the need for explanation. We belong simply because we do. "

AMY PURDY

CHANNING TATUM

THE ACTOR WHO LEARNED ON THE JOB

Growing up with dyslexia and ADHD, Channing Tatum thought he wasn't smart. He felt let down and left behind by the educational system, but he found ways to learn outside the classroom and discovered a place where he could flourish—in the arts. Today, the acclaimed actor and savvy producer is a sought-after lead whose risky independent projects have made him a huge box-office success.

NAME: *Channing Matthew Tatum*
BORN: April 26, 1980
NATIONALITY: American
PROFESSION: Actor and producer

Channing Tatum was a very high-energy kid. His mom called him "Chanimal." Constantly on the move, Channing poured his energy into sports as his family moved between Alabama, Mississippi, and Florida. He excelled at football, but the academic side of school wasn't going so well. Channing had ADHD, dyslexia, and a stutter. Never quite getting the support he needed to engage with learning, he grew up thinking he wasn't smart. When he was prescribed meds to help him focus, they made him feel like a "zombie" and sometimes hopelessly depressed. Channing won a football scholarship to a college in West Virginia, but a semester in, he realized that formal education wasn't for him. That didn't mean he was done with learning.

Channing was always curious about the world. He didn't grow up in an artistic household, but he'd always been especially interested in the arts. His mom encouraged him to "be a sponge," and he was, absorbing ideas and information from the people he encountered, learning "everything [he] could from anybody who knew something [he] didn't."

Being a sponge helped him go from dancer to model to actor very quickly. Surrounded by the arts, Channing flourished. When someone approached him on the street in Miami and asked him if he had representation, he began taking himself seriously and approached modeling agencies. He was cast as a dancer in a Ricky Martin music video, then picked up for prints ads by major fashion brands like the GAP. A Pepsi commercial and a bit part on *CSI: Miami* led to his first movie role in 2005, acting alongside Hollywood legend Samuel L. Jackson in the basketball film *Coach Carter*.

Samuel ended up being the novice actor's behind-the-scenes coach, too. Channing was worried about how to approach learning a lengthy script with his dyslexia and ADHD. Samuel advised him to stop trying to read lines and instead figure out how his part fit in with the overall conversation. It still takes Channing five times longer than most actors to read through a script, but by the end, he knows the ideas and storylines better than anyone.

After making it big with big-budget action films like *G.I. Joe: The Rise of Cobra* and *Public Enemy*, Channing went on to vary his repertoire, with rom-coms, sci-fi epics, animated films, and acclaimed dramas. He's worked with some of the most celebrated directors in the industry, from Michael Mann to Quentin Tarantino to the Coen brothers. And he has a special relationship with Oscar-winning independent filmmaker Steven Soderbergh, with whom he's done five movies. In 2012, they teamed up to make *Magic Mike*, a story—loosely based on Channing's life—about a 19 year old trying to make his way in Tampa, Florida's glitzy nightlife scene. He took a risk and self-funded the project, and it paid off. The film took $7 million to produce and earned a cool $167 million at the box office, leading to two sequels and a stage adaptation.

In 2022, the award-winning actor and producer made his directorial debut on a film in which his costar was a Belgian Malinois dog named Lulu. The arts all-arounder is also a new children's author. His endearing series, *The One and Only Sparkella*, is inspired by the life lessons he's shared with his own sparkling young "glitter poop" of a daughter, like: "Sometimes all you can do is be more you-ish."

" I GET ONE SHOT AT LIFE, AND I CAN SAY THAT I'VE LIVED A CRAZY ONE, AND I'VE PUSHED THE LIMIT ALMOST AT EVERY TURN, AND I'M SUPER PROUD OF THAT. "

CHANNING TATUM

If you've enjoyed reading these extraordinary biographies, here are some more famous people with disabilities or neurodivergence whose stories are worth exploring . . .

David Beckham, the retired world-class soccer player, has obsessive compulsive disorder (see page 47).

Singer, actor and TV personality **Selena Gomez** has lupus, an autoimmune disease.

Far-out sci fi author **Octavia Butler,** and boxer **Muhammad Ali**, known as "The Greatest," were diagnosed with dyslexia (see page 27). **Ali** had Parkinson's, too (see page 79), as does civil rights leader **Rev. Jesse Jackson**.

Florence Welch, frontwoman of the band Florence + the Machine, fashion icon **Tommy Hilfiger**, polar explorer **Ann Bancroft**, and famous lawyer and activist **Erin Brockovich** also have dyslexia (see page 27).

Olympic swimmer **Michael Phelps**; actor **Michelle Rodriguez**; and singers **Solange Knowles**, **Mel B** of The Spice Girls, and **Adam Levine** of Maroon 5 have been diagnosed with attention deficit hyperactivity disorder (ADHD, see page 11).

Celebrity chef **Jamie Oliver** has ADHD and dyslexia (see pages 11 and 27).

Nobel-winning mathematician **John Nash** (portrayed by **Russell Crowe** in the film *A Beautiful Mind*) was diagnosed with schizophrenia.

Music legend **Stevie Wonder** and **Baron David Blunkett**, a British politician who served as the UK's home secretary, are blind (see page 35).

Actor **Marlee Matlin** (youngest winner of the Academy Award for Best Actress) is deaf (see page 39).

Historic inventor **Thomas Edison** was hard of hearing, as is US president **Bill Clinton** (see page 39).

Coldplay frontman **Chris Martin** and singer-songwriter **Grimes** have tinnitus and hearing loss.

US senator and former military officer **Tammy Duckworth** is a double amputee (see page 103).

Race car driver **Nicolas Hamilton** has cerebral palsy (see page 63).

Skater and Olympic gold medalist **Kristi Yamaguchi** was born with clubfoot.

Paralympic swimmer **Ellie Simmonds** and actor **Tony Cox** have achondroplasia (see page 55).

Actors **Selma Blair** and **Christina Applegate** have multiple sclerosis (MS, see page 67).

Pop star **Lewis Capaldi** and former pro goalkeeper **Tim Howard** have Tourette's syndrome (see page 31).

Jessica Cox, the first armless licensed pilot, was born with phocomelia syndrome.

Influential anthropologist **Dawn Prince-Hughes**, Oscar-winning actor **Sir Anthony Hopkins** and comedian **Dan Aykroyd** have been diagnosed with autism spectrum disorder (see page 15).

Renowned surrealist painter **Frida Kahlo** had polio and spina bifida (see page 99).

Model Sofía Jirau, actor **Zack Gottsagen**, and gymnast **Chelsea Werner** were born with Down syndrome.

TIMELINE

1952—2004
Christopher Reeve

1958
Andrea Bocelli

1961
Michael J. Fox

1979
Amy Purdy

1980
Channing Tatum

1981
Esther Vergeer

1992
Gary Payton II

1997
Simone Biles

1997
Camila Cabello

1881—1973
Pablo Picasso

1936—1996
Barbara Jordan

1942—2018
Stephen Hawking

1947
Temple Grandin

1964
Trischa Zorn

1969
Peter Dinklage

1970
Warwick Davis

1971
Paris Hilton

1982
Nick Vujicic

1987
Ali Stroker

1991
Aaron
Fotheringham

1992
RJ Mitte

2001
Billie Eilish

2003
Greta Thunberg

2003
Millicent
Simmonds

2004
Millie Bobby
Brown

INDEX